THE AUGUST WILSON CENTURY CYCLE

JITNEY

1977

JITNEY

1977

AUGUST WILSON

FOREWORD BY ISHMAEL REED

THEATRE COMMUNICATIONS GROUP

NEW YORK

2007

The August Wilson Century Cycle is published by Theatre Communications Group, Inc.,
520 Eighth Avenue, 24th Floor, New York, NY 10018-4156

The August Wilson Century Cycle is funded in part by the Ford Foundation, with additional support from The Paul G. Allen Family Foundation, The Heinz Endowments and the New York State Council on the Arts.

TCG books are exclusively distributed to the book trade by Consortium Book Sales and Distribution, 1045 Westgate Drive, St. Paul, MN 55114.

LIBRARY OF CONGRESS CATALOGING-IN-PUBLICATION DATA
Wilson, August.
Jitney / August Wilson ; foreword by Ishmael Reed.—1st ed.
p. cm.—(August Wilson century cycle)
ISBN-13: 978-1-55936-304-4 (vol.)
ISBN-10: 1-55936-304-5 (vol.)
ISBN-13: 978-1-55936-307-5 (set)
ISBN-10: 1-55936-307-X (set)
1. Hill District (Pittsburgh, Pa.)—Drama. 2. African American neighborhoods—Drama. 3. Taxicab drivers—Drama. 4. African Americans—Drama.
5. Nineteen seventies—Drama. 6. Pittsburgh (Pa.)—Drama. I. Title.
PS3573.I45677J58 2007
812'.54—dc22   2007022089

Text design and composition by Lisa Govan
Slipcase and cover design by John Gall
Cover photograph by Danny Lyon/Magnum Photos
Slipcase photographs by Dana Lixenberg (author) and David Cooper

First Edition, September 2007

For Azula Carmen Wilson,
who burst upon the world clothed in the light of angelic grace,
you are more blessing than I deserve

FOREWORD

by Ishmael Reed

As a young man living in New York during the 1960s, I was always struck by how some critics approached the work of Soviet poet Yevgeny Yevtushenko. Most of the emphasis was placed on content and little on form. His poems were treated as intelligence about political trends within the Soviet Union, our enemy at the time.

I suspect that the same thing happens here. "What's up with the Sisters and Brothers?" seems to be the question of some critics when they are inspecting an African American writer's work, or, as Adolph Reed, Jr., put it: "What do those drums mean?" The perennial question for minority writers is: What is the motive of mainstream white critics for favoring one minority artist over the other?

I've seen plays by Adrienne Kennedy, Suzan-Lori Parks, Amiri Baraka, Thulani Davis, Aishah Rahman and August Wilson. I worked with Ed Bullins during his 1980s California sojourn during which he ran a truly grassroots theater. While New York critics seem to be able to choose the best of these playwrights or "Black America's Best Playwright" or "The Poet of Black America" or " The Country's Greatest African American Playwright," I would have difficulty doing so. Under a grant from the Lila Wallace Foundation, I accompanied Second Start adult literacy students to one play a month for three years. One of the most outstanding was Marvin X's *One Day in the Life*. I doubt whether New York critics who anoint this playwright or crown that one have ever heard of Marvin X, let alone seen his plays. That probably goes for Marie Evans and Aishah Rahman as well.

I doubt whether Robert Brustein, August Wilson's debating partner (this relationship came to a head following Wilson's incendiary speech at TCG's National Theatre Conference in 1996, and continued in *American Theatre* magazine for several issues, culminating in a standing-room-only debate at New York's Town Hall in 1997), was familiar with a number of black playwrights when he implied that black playwrights are recipients of a Theatrical Affirmative Action. (Brustein opposed Affirmative Action at Yale.) Not that Robert Brustein is a malevolent man. My partner, Carla Blank, and I had a good lunch with him when I taught at Harvard. But Brustein is like some other American critics who judge African American art on the basis of prejudices and a tiny sampling of work. I don't think it has that much to do with race. Critics in Asia, Europe and Africa have a better grasp of African American literature than white American critics. French critic Geneviève Fabre knows more about black theater than any white American scholar or critic. She's white. Moreover, Brustein seemed to be using a double standard when debating Wilson. While opposing Wilson's call for an ethnic theater, he admitted that the "roots" of his play *Nobody Dies on Friday* were in "Yiddish theater." Why is it all right for Brustein to write an ethnic play, yet oppose Wilson's call for an ethnic theater? Is Brustein saying that Yiddish plays have more universal import than black ethnic theater? During the Town Hall debate, Brustein said, in an attempt to distance himself from his ethnic roots, that though his people came from Poland, he didn't consider himself Polish. *Newsweek* critic Jack Kroll wrote: "Wilson might have answered that Brustein's heartbeats were not Polish, but Jewish."

Though their approaches to theater are radically different, Wilson says that he was influenced by Amiri Baraka. Yet the critics who praise Wilson have ignored Baraka for years. When a theater finally decided to produce a revival of Baraka's *Dutchman*, the *Times* assigned a radical, white, feminist to review it; she subsequently trashed it (this was like turning an Arab over to the guards at Gitmo). And from the writings of black critics (some who examine work by black authors as a sideline), one gains the impression that they haven't seen one of Baraka's plays since the 1960s.

Toward the end of his life, Wilson seems to have been contemplating writing a play with a more postmodernist bent. From his description, it sounded like something akin to Kennedy's *Funnyhouse of a Negro*.

Nicholas Lemann in his book *Redemption* says that white Southerners have an innate fear of a "black uprising," even though organized slave revolts historically were few. The traditional way to handle such fears has been to appoint, in the words of Paul Laurence Dunbar, "the Big Negro." Maybe the same thing happens in the world of the arts as well. I wouldn't be the first to point to the historic trend of "mainstream" critics choosing a token, like an ox with garlands around its neck, who will eventually be led to artistic slaughter. Usually, leading black academics and critics certify the choices that arrive from the literary Big House like members of a neo-colonial government rubber-stamping the choices of their imperialist masters. John A. Williams recognized this tendency some years ago. Williams is a much more polished novelist than Ralph Ellison, whom the New York intellectual machine has crowned the King of Black Novelists. But those who choose black tokens find Williams's content too strong. Or how do they say it, "controversial."

And so the question remains: Are some writers being praised because a conservative period calls for plays that don't upset what the late Lloyd Richards called the "plastic card crowd" (white middle-class theatergoers), those plays that preach individual responsibility and blame all of the problems of the black community on the behavior of black men? One can read that in Wilson's plays *Fences* and *Jitney*, where members of an older generation preach responsibility to their children whom they accuse of abandoning the values espoused by their elders. The younger generation conversely accuses the older generation of acting in a passive manner when confronted with white male aggression, which is the conflict between *Jitney*'s Booster and his dad, Becker.

One of the abiding myths of outsiders who write about black life is that the fatherless home is an exclusively black phenomenon, despite new census figures that show married families to be in the minority throughout the country. These tough-love exhortations also appear in a number of op-ed columns and books written by black and white academics and the pundit elite. It seems that white male critics welcome plays by black women in which the image of black men is similar to that found in post-Reconstruction popular culture, that of a reckless thieving rascal, misogynist and rapist.

But if Wilson was one of those writers, merely telling white people what they wanted to hear, why would he eventually break with some who had praised him? He wouldn't be the first. Langston Hughes, Claude McKay, Richard Wright, Chester Himes and Amiri Baraka had done the same. After James Baldwin rebuked those who helped him become a literary star, his sponsors (according to the late Truman Capote, in an exclusive interview printed in a magazine published by Al Young and me) treated him like "shit."

In 1997, I talked to August before he departed to New York to engage in that fateful debate with Robert Brustein.

Some unfavorable remarks had recently been made about
Wilson's theatrical abilities in the *New Republic*, a publication
in which blacks are regularly thrashed. I warned Wilson that
the debate was an ambush, that he would be subjected to a
hometown decision. I suggested he insist that the debate be
held in St. Louis. Sure enough, after the debate, the same cul-
tural machine that set up James Baldwin set him up: Wilson
was subjected to hit pieces by white supporters who deemed
him ungrateful for advocating a black nationalist theater. What
probably bothered them even more was his favorable reference
to Elijah Muhammad, the Nation of Islam leader, who had been
stereotyped by the media as a hater of white people. (In con-
nection with a book I'm writing about Muhammad Ali, I have
discovered that Elijah Muhammad often entertained whites
and Jews at his dinner table.) And from the Amen Corner, he
was hit equally as hard by black surrogates. Even Frank Rich,
the *Times* critic who was responsible for Wilson's fame, wrote:

> On the surface, Mr. Brustein, the artistic director of
> Harvard's American Repertory Theatre, won on most
> points. He argued for an integrated American culture
> that prizes multiculturalism but does not tolerate racial
> hatred or separatism or a waiving of artistic standards.
> Mr. Wilson argued for a self-segregated black theater
> in which black actors would play only black roles and
> only black writers would write about black characters.
> Even as he presented his case, it was contradicted by
> both his own career (in which he had chosen to give
> his plays to integrated, mainstream theaters) and by
> the debate's moderator, Anna Deavere Smith, the
> black artist known for her brilliant portrayals of peo-
> ple of all races and genders.

Margo Jefferson, Mr. Rich's colleague at the *Times*, wrote:

Mr. Wilson cast himself as the warrior-king of all people of African descent living in the United States. He spoke as though he embodied every experience every one of them had ever had (no one contains that many multitudes), and as though all authentic (and by implication great) black art were being forged in the smithy—or the slave ship—of his soul.

A Princeton website accused Wilson of anti-Semitism:

One reason some were disturbed was the subtle but insistent joining of Wilson's vivid evocations of genetic memories of the slave trade with such anti-Semitic code words as "financiers," and a description of black artists as "victims of the counting houses."

Perhaps the most scathing, even cruel, response to Wilson's position was written by Henry Louis Gates, Jr., for the *New Yorker*. Gates flogged Black Nationalism and the Black Arts Movement, accusing Wilson of aligning himself with those groups, whom Gates considered to be homophobic and misogynist (though gay people and women were active in both movements).

Ironically, Wilson's insistence that he was a member of a culture that had been segregated was corroborated by the *Times*, the publication whose critics took exception to his speech. In its obituary, Wilson was not called an "American playwright" but a "black playwright." August Wilson was criticized as a nationalist by those who can be the fiercest of nationalists, and criticized as a segregationist by those who, at the time of the debate (and to this day), were running a segregated arts scene.

I think the 1997 debate was his way of distancing himself from the neo-cons and neo-liberals who had claimed him as a member of their ranks. For some African Americans, including me, white conservatism is merely a euphemism for racism, because, unlike traditional conservatism, American conservatives seem to have one issue: out-of-wedlock births from the black "underclass," about which they still write op-eds and long ignorant books, even though the black teenage pregnancy rate has declined while that of white and Hispanic women is soaring.

And so, if August Wilson's plays have a conservative line, it was not to appeal to those critics who misread him, but a reflection of the attitudes of a large segment of the African American community. Wilson's conservatism was *his*, that of Booker T. Washington, Elijah Muhammad, Malcolm X and Marcus Garvey, all of whom preached self-help and individual responsibility, and all of whom did business with white people; not *theirs*, which often took the form of vicious and nasty comments about the underclass.

In his speech, "The Ground on Which I Stand" (TCG, 2001), which incited the debate, Wilson said:

> . . . the ground that I stand on has been pioneered by my grandfather, by Nat Turner, by Denmark Vesey, by Martin Delany, Marcus Garvey and the Honorable Elijah Muhammad.

It is easy to see why some neo-cons and white conservatives would regard Wilson as one of their own. Surely George Will, Hendrik Hertzberg, David Brooks and other conservatives would applaud the juicy lines that Wilson gives to Doub:

> That white man ain't paying you no mind. You ought to stop thinking like that. They been planning to tear these shacks down before you was born. You keep thinking everybody's against you and you ain't never gonna get nothing. I seen a hundred niggers too lazy to get up out the bed in the morning, talking about the white man is against them. That's just an excuse. You want to make something of your life, then the opportunity is there. You just have to shake off that

"white folks is against me" attitude. Hell, they don't even know you alive.

Since this kind of speech reoccurs in Wilson's plays, one might assume that this is his position—that anybody can make it if one works hard and takes advantages of opportunities.

Of course, it's not as simple as that. Even the Bush administration admits to the existence of racial profiling; the *New England Journal of Medicine* has documented racial disparities in health care; the Center for Responsible Lending has issued a report about the unequal treatment of blacks by the mortgage-lending institutions, even to those who work hard and play by the rules, etc. And so when the character Youngblood bought that house in Penn Hills he probably had to pay a higher interest rate than Pittsburgh whites who had the same credit rating as his. Black and white conservatives accuse blacks of wallowing in a cult of victimization. Hell, judging from the facts that I have studied, they are victims!!

While many whites are not against black people (or are indifferent to them), there are those in key positions who appear to be. Doub suggests that Youngblood use the GI Bill to attend school. Ira Katznelson writes in *When Affirmative Action Was White* (still is):

> . . . the GI Bill did create a more middle-class society, but almost exclusively for whites. Written under Southern auspices, the law was deliberately designed to accommodate Jim Crow. Its administration widened the country's racial gap.

Seems as though some of the whites who designed the GI Bill were "against" blacks.

Though Wilson says his plays are not about politics, the politics are implied. For instance, blacks don't have the power to make decisions that would determine whether a neighborhood is subjected to public domain or urban renewal, a major issue in *Jitney*. Some argue that urban renewal, by dispersing the black community, is responsible for the problems experienced in the cities. Wilson would agree that integration, which led to the separation of middle-class blacks from the so-called underclass blacks, had bad effects.

Some of the themes in *Jitney* are as contemporary as gentrification. Others are as ancient as rape, as in the Scottsboro case of the 1930s, in which some black men were falsely accused of rape. In *Jitney* also, which takes place in 1977, a white woman screams rape when her liaison with a black man, Booster, is exposed (but I doubt whether the 1960s warriors would consider Booster's murder of a rich white woman heroic; he represents the generation that the elders believe has gone astray). According to *The Trouble Between Us* by Winifred Breines, a rare look into the conflict between black and white feminists, a dirty little secret is exposed: the main complaint that black men and women had against the white women who joined Freedom Summer (a group formed in 1964 to register African Americans to vote) was that they got in the way and tried to run things. Booster's murder of a white woman who accused him of rape feels more 1930s, like Richard Wright's Bigger Thomas, a man who murders two women in *Native Son*.

Another recurrent element in his plays is the fratricidal arguments between the men. These disputes erupt over trivial incidents, but signify deeper, subterranean issues, though sometimes these issues are not dredged. In *Jitney*, people get into fights over a thirty-cent cup of coffee or a fifty-cent unpaid fare. (The *New York Times'* Fox Butterfield says that fighting over small things is a style that blacks inherited from Southern Celtics.)

But Wilson's greatest triumph is the creation of his characters. His characters are complex and human. A great ear helped. He must have spent thousands of hours tape-recording in that brilliant mind of his the back-and-forth among black male characters. The tall tales: Fielding says that he was such a good tailor that Count Basie canceled engagements to wait for a suit that he was making for him. The dreams: Booster says that he could have become a heavyweight champion or Albert Einstein. The arguments: The beauty of Lena Horne versus that of Sarah Vaughan. Wilson captures the small talk as well as the philosophical musings and poetry that go on whenever black men gather.

I don't know where August got his Blues from. He says he listened to records. You can listen to all the records you wish, but that doesn't guarantee you'll be successful in getting the Blues down on paper. Wilson has to rank with Langston Hughes and Ernest Gaines as a writer—his ear was so good that his characters' words could be set to music. Shealy's monologue in the first scene of *Jitney* is an example. Not only did August excel stylistically in bringing the Blues to paper, but all of the *issues* of the Blues are presented in this play as well.

Since I signed up with XM-Satellite radio, I've been able to listen to the Blues whenever I wish. Sexual jealousy, especially songs that address a lover's absence (usually about women staying out all night and, the worst, coming home the next morning with bloodshot eyes), money, betrayal, death, getting drunk, the boasting about material possessions (especially automobiles, specifically Cadillacs) seem to be the main themes. Sometimes they are soul-wrenching cries like Ray Charles's "Sinner's Prayer." Sometimes serious events like death are treated humorously: "Don't Send Me Flowers When I'm in the Graveyard." But there are also good-time songs: "I Ain't Drunk, I'm Just Drinkin'," "Gimmie a Pigfoot and a Bottle of Beer." In *Jitney*, one character says that the two issues that can get you killed are money and women. Wilson has the Blues covered.

Ishmael Reed is a poet, novelist, playwright, librettist, essayist, song writer and publisher. He made his debut as a jazz pianist and group leader with the CD For All We Know, *recorded by The Ishmael Reed Quintet in 2007.*

JITNEY

1977

Jitney had its world premiere in October 1982, at the Allegheny Repertory Theatre in Pittsburgh. It was then presented in 1985, by the Penumbra Theatre Company in St. Paul, Minnesota. Subsequent productions of a revised version of *Jitney* were performed at the following theaters: Pittsburgh Public Theater, Pittsburgh, June 1996; Crossroads Theatre Company, New Brunswick, New Jersey, April 1997; Huntington Theatre Company, Boston, October 1998; CENTERSTAGE, Baltimore, January 1999; Studio Arena Theatre, Buffalo, New York, March 1999; Geva Theatre Center, Rochester, New York, April 1999; The Goodman Theatre, Chicago, June 1999; Center Theatre Group's Mark Taper Forum, Los Angeles, January 2000.

Jitney had its New York premiere on April 25, 2000, at the Second Stage Theatre (Carole Rothman, Artistic Director; Alexander Fraser, Executive Director; Carol Fishman, Managing Director). It was directed by Marion McClinton; the set design was by David Gallo, the costume design was by Susan Hilferty, the lighting design was by Donald Holder, the sound design was by Rob Milburn; the production stage manager was Narda Alcorn. The cast was as follows:

YOUNGBLOOD	Russell Hornsby
TURNBO	Stephen McKinley Henderson
FIELDING	Anthony Chisholm
DOUB	Barry Shabaka Henley
SHEALY	Willis Burks II
PHILMORE	Leo V. Finnie III
BECKER	Paul Butler
BOOSTER	Carl Lumbly
RENA	Michole Briana White

CHARACTERS

YOUNGBLOOD, jitney driver and Vietnam veteran. Mid to late twenties.

TURNBO, jitney driver who is always interested in the business of others.

FIELDING, jitney driver and former tailor, with a dependency on alcohol.

DOUB, longtime jitney driver and Korean War veteran.

SHEALY, numbers taker who often uses the jitney station as his base.

PHILMORE, local hotel doorman, recurring jitney passenger.

BECKER, well-respected man who runs the jitney station. Sixties.

BOOSTER, Becker's son, recently released from prison. Early forties.

RENA, Youngblood's girlfriend and mother of their young son.

ACT ONE

SCENE I

The time is early fall, 1977. The setting is a gypsy cab station in Pittsburgh, Pennsylvania. The paint is peeling off the walls, and the floor is covered with linoleum that is worn through in several areas. In the middle of the wall stage left sits an old-fashioned pot-bellied stove that dominates the room. Upstage of it is a blackboard on which is written the rates to different parts of the city, and the daily, marginally illegal policy numbers. Next to the blackboard a sign reads: "Becker's Rules: 1. No overcharging; 2. Keep car clean; 3. No drinking; 4. Be courteous; 5. Replace and clean tools." Downstage on the wall is a pay phone. The entire right wall is made up of the entrance down right and a huge picture window. Along the upstage wall is a couch, with several chairs of various styles and ages scattered about to complete the setting.

As the scene opens it is mid-morning. Youngblood and Turnbo sit facing each other on folding chairs in front of the couch. They are playing checkers, with the checkerboard on their knees in front of them. Fielding sits in a chair down left.

YOUNGBLOOD (*Agitated*): Naw! You can't do that! How you gonna take my man?

TURNBO: I'm gonna jump him, fool!

YOUNGBLOOD: How you gonna jump him with the man sitting there! I got a man sitting there! Is you blind?

TURNBO: Well, put him where he belongs then! I ain't seen him sitting there. I thought he was on the other square.

(*He studies the board and makes his move. Youngblood jumps his man.*)

YOUNGBLOOD: Don't you know I was the checker champ of 'Nam.

TURNBO: Boy, ain't nobody studying you. (*Moves*) There! Champ that!

(*Fielding eases a half-pint bottle of gin from under the cushion of the chair. Discovering it is empty, he eases it back.*)

YOUNGBLOOD (*Studying the board*): I done told you who you playing with now. Can't nobody beat me. I'm like Muhammad Ali. I'm the greatest!

FIELDING (*Gets up suddenly*): Youngblood, let me have four dollars. I got to go.

TURNBO (*Does a double jump*): Come on and move, checker champ! What's the matter now? Huh?

YOUNGBLOOD: I ain't got it, Fielding. If I had it you know I'd give it to you.

TURNBO: Come on and play, checker champ.

FIELDING: Turnbo, let me have four dollars.

TURNBO (*To Youngblood, agitated*): Will you come on and move, man!

FIELDING: Let me have the four dollars.

TURNBO: Fielding, you know better than to ask me for anything.

(*Youngblood moves, and Turnbo jumps two of his men.*)

King me! King me! Come on, checker champ, let me beat you again.

(*The phone rings.*)

YOUNGBLOOD: No, you cheat, old man.
FIELDING (*Answering the phone*): Car service. (*Pause*) East Liberty? Whereabouts in East Liberty? (*Pause*) That'll be four dollars. (*Pause*) Lady, I don't care what nobody else charge you that's a four-dollar trip. (*Pause*) All right. Green car. What's the address again? (*Pause*) I'll be right there.

(*He hangs up as Doub enters.*)

Doub, let me have four dollars.
DOUB: What?
FIELDING: I got to make a run to East Liberty. Give me four dollars, I'll give it back to you.
DOUB: Hell, nigger, I ain't no bank.
FIELDING: Aw, give me the four dollars. I got to get some gas.
TURNBO: If you don't go out and drink up your money you'd have four dollars and wouldn't have to be asking nobody.
FIELDING: Ain't nobody ask you what I do with my money. (*To Doub*) Let me have the four dollars, I'll give it back to you.
DOUB (*Going into his pocket*): Here . . . here . . . don't ask me for nothing else. This is your one time in life to ask me for something. (*Hands Fielding the money*) You bring my four dollars back here too.

(*Fielding exits.*)

TURNBO: Fielding ain't gonna do nothing but drink up that money. He going right out there to the State Store.

(*The phone rings.*)

YOUNGBLOOD (*Answering the phone*): Car service. (*Pause*) Giant Eagle? Wait a minute, you gotta get somebody else.

TURNBO: Here . . . I'll take it. (*Takes the phone*) Yeah? Which Giant Eagle? (*Pause*) All right. Be right there. Brown car. You already checked out and ready to go 'cause I ain't gonna be waiting. (*Pause*) Okay. (*Exits*)

(*Doub watches Youngblood.*)

YOUNGBLOOD: What you looking at me for?

DOUB: I ain't said nothing to you.

YOUNGBLOOD: I ain't gonna mess up my car hauling people's groceries around.

DOUB: What you telling me for? I don't care about your business. Becker's the one you ought to be telling what you is and ain't gonna do.

(*Shealy enters.*)

SHEALY: How's everybody in here?

YOUNGBLOOD: Hey Shealy.

DOUB: I see your boy down the street got a brand-new car.

YOUNGBLOOD: Who? Who got a new car?

DOUB: Pope who own that restaurant down on Centre.

YOUNGBLOOD: What'd he get?

DOUB: He got a brand-new shiny Buick Riviera. How much did he hit for, Shealy?

SHEALY: You know me, Doub. I don't be putting nobody's business in the street. First thing you know somebody be done got killed talking about "Shealy said . . ." I ain't gonna have that on my conscience. I don't know nothing.

DOUB: I know he hit big. He been playing that two sixty-one every day for years.

SHEALY: I don't know nothing about it . . . but I do know he's closing up his restaurant. The city's tearing it down.

DOUB: They gonna tear it down before it fall down.

YOUNGBLOOD: I didn't know you and Pope was tight.

SHEALY: We ain't tight. I don't know why Doub wanna tie me up with him.

DOUB: Oh now . . . I remember when you all used to be tight.

SHEALY: Must be when he had that little yellow gal working for him. That's the only time you ever see me down there.

DOUB: What ever happened to that gal?

SHEALY: She married to one of them boys that drive a bus. That's what I hear.

DOUB: She wasn't the one, huh?

SHEALY: Naw, she wasn't the one. I thought she was but then I believe Rosie done put a curse on me. She don't want me to have no other woman. But then she didn't want me. I told her, baby, just tell me what kind of biscuits you want to make. I'm like the mill-man, I can grind it up any way you want. She knew I was telling the truth too. She couldn't say nothing about that. She say you a poor man. What I need with a poor man? I told her say if I make a hundred I'll give you ninety-nine. She didn't trust me on that one but I went down to the crap game, hit six quick licks, left with a hundred and sixty-three dollars. I went on back up there. She let me in. I lay a hundred dollars down on the table and told her, "Now, if I can just get one of them back I'd be satisfied." She reached down and handed me a dollar and I went on in the room and went to bed. Got up and she had my breakfast on the table. It wasn't soon long that ninety-nine dollars ran out and next thing I knew she had barred the door. I went on and left but I never could get her off my mind. I said I was gonna find me another woman. But every time I get hold to one . . . time I lay down with them . . . I see Rosie's face. I told myself the first time I lay down with a woman and don't see her face then that be the one I'm gonna marry. That be my little test. Now with that little yellow gal used to work down at

Pope's I seen Rosie's face . . . but it was blurry. Like a cloud or something come over it. I say, "I got to try this again. Maybe next time I won't see nothing." She told me she didn't want to see me no more. She told me come back same time tomorrow and if she changed her mind she'd leave the key in the mailbox. I went up there and there was one man in the house and two others sitting on the doorstep. I don't know who had the key.

(The phone rings.)

YOUNGBLOOD *(Answering the phone)*: Car service. *(Pause)* Yeah. Shealy.
SHEALY *(Taking the phone)*: Shealy here. *(Takes out a pad and pencil and begins writing)*
YOUNGBLOOD: I'm going next door to Clifford's. *(Exits)*
SHEALY *(Into the phone)*: Six seventy-one straight. Four sixty-nine boxed for a dollar. I got it. I'll see you down Irv's later on. *(Hangs up the phone)* You ain't seen Becker, have you?
DOUB: He was by here earlier this morning. I think he had to make a run to take care of some business.
SHEALY: You know his boy getting out of the penitentiary next month.

(The phone rings.)

DOUB: No kidding.
SHEALY: After all them years.
DOUB: Time go along and it come around.
SHEALY: It don't never stop.
DOUB *(Answering the phone)*: Car service. *(Pause)* Where? *(Pause)* Be right there. Blue car. *(Hangs up the phone)* Shealy, give me a dollar on that six seventy-four, I'll give it to you when I get back. *(Exits)*

(Shealy sits in a chair and goes over his number slips. Philmore enters.)

SHEALY: Hey, Philmore.

PHILMORE: Ain't no cars here?

SHEALY: Doub just left . . . he be back in a minute.

PHILMORE: I got to get home. I been out all night and half the morning. My old lady gonna be mad at me.

SHEALY: You been out all night, huh?

PHILMORE: I went down the Workmen's Club. They had Kenny Fisher down there. You couldn't hardly get in. I ain't never seen so many people. You used to have to have a job to get in there.

SHEALY: I know they glad they changed that rule. Wouldn't nobody be down there.

PHILMORE: I'd be down there. I got me a job.

SHEALY: I know. You work down the hotel. You been there a while.

PHILMORE: Six years. I been down there six years. Started May sixteen, nineteen seventy-one. Been down there six years and ain't never missed a day. And I ain't never been late. I'm supposed to get a raise. My old lady told me when I get my raise she was gonna . . .

(*Youngblood enters.*)

SHEALY: There go Youngblood.

PHILMORE: Come on, take me home. I got to get home. My old lady gonna be mad at me.

YOUNGBLOOD: Where you live at?

PHILMORE: You know where I live at. Everybody know where I live at. I live out there above the Frankstown Bar.

YOUNGBLOOD: That's a four-dollar trip. You got four dollars?

PHILMORE: Look here . . . let me show you something. Watch this. (*Builds a pyramid out of dollar bills, then blows them over*) Now when my old lady tells me I been out blowing my money . . . you can tell her it's the truth.

YOUNGBLOOD (*Laughing*): You see this, Shealy?

PHILMORE: Shealy done seen me do that before.
SHEALY: Go on, Philmore!

(*Youngblood and Philmore exit. The phone rings.*)

(*Answering the phone*) Yeah? (*Pause*) Who? (*Pause*) Naw, Mr. Becker ain't here. Who? (*Pause*) Let me see if I got this. Mr. Pease. Pittsburgh Renewal Council. Yeah, I'll tell him.

(*Turnbo enters.*)

TURNBO: Boy, I don't know what this world's coming to. You know McNeil, don't you?
SHEALY: Who?
TURNBO: McNeil! McNeil what live up on Webster. Old Lady McNeil, got them two boys and work cleaning up down at the courthouse.
SHEALY (*Trying to recognize the name*): McNeil? I don't know . . .
TURNBO (*Agitated*): You know who I'm talking about! McNeil! Use to be Brownie's old lady. You know Brownie was staying up there trying to help her raise them two boys. One of them got an old funny-shaped head.
SHEALY: Oh, yeah. Yeah, I know who you talking about now.
TURNBO: Well, the boy come by here a little while ago this morning. The oldest one, can't be no more than sixteen or seventeen at the most. Come by here and asked me to carry him on a trip to the Northside. Then he say he got to make a stop up on Whiteside Road. I carried him up there and he go into one of them houses and come on out carrying a television. He ain't said nothing about no television now. I told him it was gonna cost him two dollars more for me to be hauling around a television. Had me carry him over on the Northside to the pawnshop.

Now, I know the boy done stole the television, but I ain't said nothing. I just want my money. Come on back and stopped at Pat's Place to get me some tobacco, and the fellows standing around just happened to mention the name of this woman who done had her television stolen. Don't you know that boy done went and stole his grandmama's television! Name is Bolger. Miss Sarah Bolger. That's old lady McNeil's mother. I used to carry her to church before she got too old to go. Steal his own grandmother's television!

SHEALY: That ain't nothing, Turnbo. I seen worse than that.

(Becker enters.)

TURNBO: Yeah, I have too. But what would make someone want to steal their grandmama's television? I can't figure it out. Becker, you know McNeil what live up on Webster used to be Brownie's old lady . . . work cleaning up at the courthouse . . . got them two boys . . . one of them got an old funny-shaped head . . .

BECKER: I don't want to hear that, Turnbo. I got other things on my mind. *(To Shealy)* Here's Lucille's numbers. I hear Pope done hit.

SHEALY: Yeah. He hit pretty big. Say Becker, I been meaning to ask you. I got a nephew that's trying to make something of himself. You reckon you be able to get him on down at the mill?

BECKER: I don't know if they hiring. But I'll check into it. I know some people down there will be able to take care of him if they hiring. I can't promise nothing but I'll talk to them for you.

SHEALY: Thanks, Becker. His name is Robert Shealy. He's trying to straighten himself out and I told his mama I'd check around and see what I can do. Thanks again. Here go your message.

(Shealy hands Becker a piece of a page, then exits.)

TURNBO: You don't know nothing about Shealy's nephew, I can tell that. Boy's the biggest rogue . . . what you call a thug . . . you ever seen. He done been down there in the workhouse. Him and Jenkin's boy is the ones what broke into Taylor's bar.

BECKER: Turnbo, ain't nobody asked you nothing. You just like an old lady, always gossiping and running off at the mouth.

TURNBO: I'm just talking what I know.

(The phone rings. Doub enters.)

DOUB: Say Becker, I see you got some new tires.

BECKER: Yeah, I got two. Gonna get two more next week. *(Answering the phone)* Car service. *(Pause)* Wooster Street. *(Pause)* Yeah I know where it's at. Black car.

(Youngblood enters as Becker exits.)

YOUNGBLOOD: Cigar Annie standing up there in the middle of Robert Street cussing out everybody.

DOUB: Oh, yeah. Who she mad at now?

YOUNGBLOOD: She started with God and went on down the list. She cussing out the mayor, Doc Goldblum, Mr. Eli, her landlord, the light man, gas man, telephone man, and anybody else she can think of. They got her furniture and everything sitting out on the sidewalk.

TURNBO: I knew it was gonna come to that. Everybody else done moved out of that place two months ago. The building been condemned for two years.

YOUNGBLOOD: She standing up there in the middle of the street raising up her dress.

TURNBO: I bet she ain't got no drawers on.

YOUNGBLOOD: She had traffic backed up . . . almost got hit by a milk truck . . . the cars trying to go around her but she won't let them. Standing there just throwing up her dress.

TURNBO: I don't know what she doing that for. She ain't got nothing nobody want. Now if Pearline get out there and raise up her dress . . . that be another thing. You have a riot on your hands. They ought to put Cigar Annie in Mayview. Her and Stool Pigeon both.

DOUB: Ain't nothing wrong with Cigar Annie. They had her down in Mayview two or three times. They figure anybody cuss out God and don't care who's listening got to be crazy. They found out she got more sense than they do. That's why they let her go. She raising up her dress 'cause that's all anybody ever wanted from her since she was twelve years old. She say if that's all you want . . . here it is.

TURNBO: She sending out an SOS. That's what she's doing.

DOUB: Turnbo, I don't know why I try and talk with you. Next time remind me to shut up.

YOUNGBLOOD: Say Doub, Peaches been by here?

DOUB: I ain't seen her.

YOUNGBLOOD: I'll be over at Clifford's if she comes.

DOUB: When you gonna work on my car? I thought you was gonna take a look at my car.

YOUNGBLOOD: I can't do it today. I'll take a look at it for you tomorrow.

TURNBO: If you going next door bring me back a cup of coffee.

YOUNGBLOOD: I ain't your slave. Walk over and get you own coffee. (*Exits*)

TURNBO: That boy ain't got no sense.

DOUB: He all right. He's just young. Got a lot to learn. That gal keep after him, he'll be all right.

TURNBO: He don't need that gal. Don't know how to treat her. Treat her like the kind of class he is.

DOUB: You don't know what nobody need. Let that boy alone to live his life. Ain't nobody told you what you need. Always talking about somebody.

TURNBO: That ain't what I'm saying. You know that gal gonna see past that boy and go on to somebody got some sense to treat her right. Somebody that got more respect for her than to be messing around with her own sister.

DOUB: You don't know what you talking about.

TURNBO: You see he be asking about her. I seen her riding around in his car here lately. She come by here and they go off running around together. Don't even try to hide it.

DOUB: That don't mean nothing 'cause she was riding in his car.

TURNBO: He be calling her on the telephone too! I know what I'm talking about. You watch. That gal is gonna see right past him.

DOUB: Well, let him find that out. He's got his own way to come to things. That's all I'm saying. Let the boy alone.

TURNBO: I ain't messing with him. I just say he ain't got no sense. I believe he got shell-shocked over there in Vietnam.

DOUB: Turnbo, you mess with anybody you get the chance to put your nose in their business. Let the boy live his life.

TURNBO: Remember that boy that used to be around here? What was his name . . . Jasper! That's it. Fool went crazy and jumped off the Irene Kaufmann Settlement House? I told you about him when I first seen him. I told you then he ain't had no sense and I'm telling you about this boy now, and you wanna call it putting my nose in folks' business. But you mark my words. I just live and let live, but damn if I can't talk to express an opinion same as everybody else, without folks accusing me of being tied up in folks' business. I just talk what I know. Just like I told you Fielding wasn't coming back with your four dollars. He out somewhere getting drunk. I told you not to give it to him.

DOUB: See, there you go, messing in people's business.

(The phone rings.)

I ain't give him nothing. I loaned him four dollars and you done already got you nose stuck up in it. That's my business about when he pay me.

16

TURNBO: I just say . . .

DOUB: Yeah, well just say it to yourself. *(Exits)*

TURNBO *(Answering the phone)*: Car service. *(Pause)* Where? *(Pause)* All right. Brown car. You be ready 'cause I ain't waiting.

(Youngblood enters carrying a cup of coffee.)

YOUNGBLOOD: Here.

TURNBO: What's that for?

YOUNGBLOOD: That's your coffee, nigger. Give me thirty cents.

TURNBO: You told me to get my own. How you know I ain't sent somebody else?

YOUNGBLOOD: Aw, nigger, take this coffee and give me thirty cents.

TURNBO: I got a trip.

(Turnbo exits. Youngblood sets the coffee down on the stove. The phone rings.)

YOUNGBLOOD *(Answering the phone)*: Car service. *(Pause)* Where you at? I thought you was going down to the furniture store with me. *(Pause)* What's wrong with your hair? Ain't nothing wrong *(Pause)* with your hair. Rudy say something was wrong with your hair? *(Pause)* Naw, I ain't told her. I'm gonna wait till everything's settled. What time you gonna be done? *(Pause)* All right, I'll pick you up at three o'clock. *(Hangs up the phone and dials again)* Mr. Harper, please. *(Pause)* Darnell Williams. *(Pause)* Mr. Harper? This is Darnell Williams . . . I'm calling about the house under the GI Bill . . . you said to call and get a closing date. *(Pause)* A title search? I thought they had the title. *(Pause)* No, I can understand that but I thought all of that was taken care of by the down payment? *(Pause)* Well, how much? *(Pause)* That's all I have to do? Ain't nothing else gonna come up? *(Pause)* Two weeks! It take that long?

(*Pause*) No, there's no doubt I'll have it for you tomorrow. Yessir, I'll have it.

(*He hangs up the phone. He takes out his notebook, looking to see how much money he has. It is obvious he does not have enough. He sits thinking when suddenly an idea occurs to him. He gets up and exits. The lights go down on the scene.*)

SCENE 2

The lights come up on the jitney station, early afternoon. Becker sits at his desk reading a newspaper. Turnbo sits downstage of him, reading a Playboy *magazine. He holds the magazine up for Becker to see.*

TURNBO: Look at this one, Becker.

BECKER (*Barely looking up*): Yeah.

TURNBO: Boy, what a man wouldn't do with that! If I get up to heaven and she ain't there, I'm gonna ask God to send me straight to hell.

(*Youngblood enters.*)

YOUNGBLOOD: Turnbo, give me my thirty cents.

TURNBO: What thirty cents you talking about?

YOUNGBLOOD: For the coffee. You know what I'm talking about.

(*Turnbo motions to the coffee on the stove.*)

TURNBO: There it is. I ain't touched it. That's your coffee.

YOUNGBLOOD: I know you better give me my thirty cents.

TURNBO: Boy, I ain't studying you.

YOUNGBLOOD (*In disbelief*): You asked me to get you some coffee and now you ain't gonna pay me?

BECKER: Give the man his money, Turnbo.

TURNBO: I ain't giving him nothing.

BECKER: I ain't gonna have that dissension in here. Give the man his money!

(*Turnbo goes into his pocket.*)

TURNBO: Here. Here's your thirty cents. (*Throws it on the floor*)

YOUNGBLOOD (*Standing over Turnbo, angry*): Pick it up!

TURNBO: It's yours. You pick it up.

YOUNGBLOOD: I ain't threw it down there.

TURNBO: Well, let it lay there then. I'm through with it.

(*Turnbo goes back to reading his magazine. Youngblood backs off.*)

YOUNGBLOOD: Well, let it lay there then. But before this day is over you gonna pick up my thirty cents.

(*Turnbo suddenly jumps up and picks up the money.*)

TURNBO: Here! Here! Here's your thirty cents. You satisfied?

(*They stare at each other for a beat. The phone rings. Youngblood moves to answer it. Turnbo moves behind him.*)

That's my trip!

BECKER: You know that's his trip, Turnbo.

TURNBO: I thought he just come back from a trip.

YOUNGBLOOD (*Answering the phone*): Car service.

BECKER: He had to go downtown to take care of some business. You know everything else I'm surprised you didn't know that.

YOUNGBLOOD: Yeah, okay. Red Chevy. (*Exits*)

TURNBO: That boy ain't got good sense.

BECKER: If you leave it to you, ain't nobody got no sense.

TURNBO: They ain't! What sense it make for that McNeil boy to steal his grandmama's television? What sense it make for Shealy's nephew to break in Taylor's bar? What sense it make for that boy to run with his girlfriend's sister? Half these niggers around here running on empty and that boy at the top of the list.

(Becker throws the newspaper down on the couch and starts for the door.)

BECKER: Turnbo, sometimes you act like a kid. If Lucille call tell her I'm picking up the groceries. If you pass a car wash you might want to stop in and get your car washed. What sense it make to haul people around in a dirty car? *(Exits)*

(Turnbo goes back to reading his magazine. The phone rings.)

TURNBO *(Answering the phone)*: Car service. Youngblood? He ain't here. Who's this? Peaches? *(Pause)* Yeah, I thought that was you. Naw, Youngblood ain't here. Is there anything you want me to tell him? *(Pause)* Pick you up at four o'clock instead of three. Okay I'll tell him.

(Rena enters.)

RENA: Mr. Turnbo, Darnell around here?
TURNBO: He went on a trip.
RENA: He say when he's coming back?
TURNBO: He'll be back in a minute. You may as well wait on him. How you doing? You don't come by too much no more. I remember you used to come by and see Young-blood . . . get some money to buy the baby some milk. He getting big I bet. How old is he now?
RENA: Two. Going on three. Running around, trying to talk.
TURNBO: Time just keep going. It don't wait on nobody. Every-thing change. I remember when you was wearing diapers. Your mother did a good job of raising you. You can tell that right off. Your mother can be proud of you. It ain't

easy these days to raise a child. I don't know what's in these young boys' heads. Seem like they don't respect nobody. They don't even respect themselves. When I was coming along that was the first thing you learned. If you didn't respect yourself . . . quite naturally you couldn't respect nobody else. When I was coming along the more respect you had for other people . . . the more people respected you. Seem like it come back to you double.

These young boys don't know nothing about that . . . and it's gonna take them a lifetime to find out. They disrespect everybody and don't think nothing about it. They steal their own grandmother's television. Get hold of one woman . . . time another one walk by they grab hold to her. Don't even care who it is. It could be anybody. I just try to live and let live. My grandmother was like that. She the one raised me. She didn't care what nobody else done as long as it didn't cross her path. She was a good woman. She taught me most everything I know. She wouldn't let you lie. That was just about the worst thing you could be. A liar didn't know the truth and wasn't never gonna find out. And everybody know it's the truth what set you free. Now I ain't trying to get in your business or nothing. Like I say, I just live and let live. But some things just come up on you wrong and you have to say something about it otherwise it throw your whole life off balance.

I know you don't want to hear this . . . but you don't need no hot-headed young boy like Youngblood. What you need is somebody level-headed who know how to respect and appreciate a woman . . . I can see the kind of woman you is. You ain't the kind of woman for Youngblood and he ain't the kind of man for you. You need a more mature . . . responsible man.

RENA: I don't think so.

TURNBO: You just wait a while. You'll see that I'm right. I done seen many a young girl wake up when it's too late. Don't you be like that. You go on and find yourself a man that know how to treat you. You don't need nobody run the streets all hours of the day and night. You ain't that kind of woman.

RENA: Darnell don't run the streets. I don't know what you talking about.

TURNBO: Oh, I see him . . . running around with other women. I see him with your sister all the time. (*The phone rings*) Day and night.

RENA: Your phone's ringing.

TURNBO: I ain't trying to get in your business now. I'm telling you this for your own good. If you was some other kind of woman, I wouldn't be wasting my time.

RENA: I got to go. Tell Darnell I was by to see him. (*Exits*)

TURNBO (*Answering the phone*): Car service. (*Pause*) Becker? Oh, hello, Lucille. He's not here right now. He said to tell you he was going to pick up some groceries. Okay, I'll tell him.

(*Doub enters.*)

DOUB: Fielding been back here?

TURNBO: I ain't seen him. I told you he laid up somewhere drunk on your four dollars. You ain't gonna see him till he sober.

(*Youngblood enters.*)

YOUNGBLOOD: Man, these white folks is slick. (*The phone rings*) They think of all kind of ways to get your money.

DOUB: If you just now finding that out . . . then God help what you don't know.

(*Rena enters.*)

RENA: Darnell, I want to see you.

YOUNGBLOOD: What you want to see me about. I'm working, woman. I told you about coming by my work.

DOUB: Your trip, Turnbo.

TURNBO: Naw it ain't!

DOUB: I just come back, nigger, take this trip!

TURNBO (*Reluctantly answering the phone*): Car service. (*Pause*) Okay. Brown car. You be ready now, 'cause I ain't gonna wait.

(*Turnbo exits, followed by Doub.*)

RENA: Darnell, I don't understand. I try so hard. I'm doing everything I can to try and make this work.

YOUNGBLOOD: What? What's the matter?

RENA: I'm working my little job down there at the restaurant . . . going to school . . . trying to take care of Jesse . . . trying to take care of your needs . . . trying to keep the house together . . . trying to make everything better. Now, I come home from work I got to go to the store. I go upstairs and look in the drawer and the food money is gone. Now you explain that to me. There was eighty dollars in the drawer that ain't in there now.

YOUNGBLOOD: I needed it. I'm gonna put it back.

RENA: What you need it for? You tell me. What's more important than me and Jesse eating?

YOUNGBLOOD: I had to pay a debt. I'm gonna put it back.

RENA: You know I don't touch the grocery money. Whatever happens, we got to eat. If I need clothes . . . I do without. My little personal stuff . . . I do without. If I ain't got no electricity . . . I do without . . . but I don't never touch the grocery money. 'Cause I'm not gonna be that irresponsible to my child. 'Cause he depend on me. I'm not going to be that irresponsible to my family. I ain't gonna be like that. Jesse gonna have a chance at life. He ain't going to school hungry 'cause I spent the grocery money on some nail polish or some Afro Sheen. He ain't gonna be laying up in the bed hungry and unable to sleep 'cause his daddy took the grocery money to pay a debt.

YOUNGBLOOD: Aw, woman, I try and do what's right and this is what I get.

RENA: You know what you be doing better than I but whatever it is it ain't enough.

YOUNGBLOOD: What you talking about now? I told you I'm gonna put the money back.

RENA: It ain't all about the money, Darnell. I'm talking about the way you been doing. You ain't never home no more.

YOUNGBLOOD: I be working. You know I'm out here hustling. I got two jobs, looking for three.

RENA: You be out half the night. I wake up and you ain't there.

YOUNGBLOOD: That's what time the people say come to work! Two A.M. to six A.M. I can't tell UPS what to do! What time to have people come to work. I told you that when I took the job. I told you that I wouldn't be home. You said okay. Now you wanna come with this about me not being home. You know where I'm at.

RENA: You say you working at UPS but I don't never see no UPS money.

YOUNGBLOOD: I had some debts to pay. I told you that too. I told you I wouldn't see no money for a while.

RENA: What kind of debt?

YOUNGBLOOD: Look baby, just hang with me a while. That's all I ask. Just for a minute.

RENA: I been hanging with you! That's what you said last time. "Hang with me and it'll all turn around." When's it gonna turn around, Darnell?

YOUNGBLOOD: Soon, baby. Soon. Just hang with me.

RENA: I just want you to know I ain't no fool, Darnell. I know you been running around with Peaches and her crowd all hours of the night. Doing whatever you be doing. I may not know everything but I know something's going on. I know you all doing something.

YOUNGBLOOD: Who told you that? Me and Peaches doing what?

RENA: She's my sister, Darnell. Don't you think I can tell she's trying to hide something from me?

YOUNGBLOOD: Hide what? What you talking about? Hide what? What she trying to hide?

RENA: Ain't no need in you bothering to come home 'cause I just might not be there when you get there. (*Exits*)

(*The phone rings. Youngblood starts to go after Rena, changes his mind and comes back. He stands in the middle of the room, perplexed. Suddenly he takes his notebook from his pocket and throws it on the floor. He regains his composure, picks up the book and exits. Becker enters on the fourth ring.*)

BECKER (*Answering the phone*): Car service. (*Pause*) Shealy don't work here!

(*Becker slams the phone down as Doub enters.*)

DOUB: I was just talking to Clifford next door. He say the man is gonna board his place up next month.

BECKER: Yeah, I know. The man from the city was by here two weeks ago too. They're gonna tear it all down, this whole block.

DOUB: The man was by here and you ain't told nobody! What he say?

BECKER: They're gonna board the place up first of next month.

DOUB: Why in the hell didn't you tell somebody!

BECKER: I'm telling you now.

DOUB: Fine time to tell me, two weeks later. It ain't like that's a small piece of news. I got rent to pay. Doctor bills. Every man in here depending on this station for their livelihood. The city's gonna board it up . . . you've known for two weeks . . . and you ain't bothered to get around to telling nobody. That ain't like you, Becker. What we gonna do now? In the two weeks we got.

BECKER: I don't know. I kinda figured we'd all just go in together somewhere else. Find another place. But I don't know now. I'm just tired, Doub. Can't hardly explain it none. You look up one day and all you got left is what you ain't spent. Every day cost you something and you don't all the time realize it.

I used to question God about everything. Why he hardened Pharaoh's heart? Why he let Jacob steal his brother's birthright? After Coreen died I told myself I wasn't gonna ask no more questions. 'Cause the answers didn't matter. They didn't matter right then. I thought that would change but it never did. It still don't matter after all these years. It don't look like it's never gonna matter. I'm tired of waiting for God to decide whether he want to hold my hand. I been running cars out of here for eighteen years and I think I'm just tired of driving.

DOUB: I been with you for twelve of them eighteen years and I would have thought you would have told me we was gonna have to move 'cause they boarding up the station.

BECKER: I'm telling you now.

DOUB: That ain't what I mean, Becker. It's like you just a shadow of yourself. The station done gone downhill. Some people overcharge. Some people don't haul. Fielding stay drunk. I just watch you and you don't do nothing.

BECKER: What's to be done? I try to keep cars running out of here and keep everybody happy. I post the rates up on the board. If somebody charge extra and people complain, I give them the difference and tell the driver about it. I ain't gonna put nobody out unless they totally irresponsible. As for Fielding, I don't let him drink in here, but I can't tell the man about his personal business unless people start to complain.

DOUB: Complain? Hell, they don't do no complaining. They just call somebody else. Somebody ask them for a number, they don't give them Court 1-9802. They give them somebody else's number. Complain? You think they're gonna call you up and complain? Nigger, they don't even know you're alive.

BECKER: I just do the best I can do.

DOUB: Sometime your best ain't enough.

(*Turnbo enters.*)

Turnbo, they boarding up the station the first of the month. Becker talking about quitting, so we ought to start thinking about moving somewhere or getting on with somebody else.

TURNBO: Who's boarding up the station?

DOUB: The city. They fixing to tear down the whole block. Clifford and everybody done got their notices. The man was by here two weeks ago.

TURNBO: So that's what they was doing! I seen them snooping around here. Told me they was conducting a survey. Well, what we gonna do? Becker, you quitting?

BECKER: I ain't said I was quitting.

DOUB: That's what you told me.

BECKER: I said I was thinking about it.

(*The phone rings.*)

DOUB: We ought to have a meeting and figure out one way or another what we gonna do.

TURNBO: They never could leave well enough alone. (*Answering the phone*) Car service. (*Pause*) Oh hello, Lucille, he's here. Just a minute. Becker! (*Hands Becker the phone*) They won't be satisfied until they tear the whole goddamn neighborhood down!

BECKER (*Into the phone*): Becker here. (*Pause*) Yeah, I know, Lucille. (*Pause*) Tomorrow? I thought it wasn't until next month. Who called? (*Pause*) Are you sure? (*Pause*) Yeah, well okay. I'll talk to you. (*Hangs up the phone*)

TURNBO: They gonna board up the place tomorrow!

BECKER: My boy's getting out tomorrow.

(*The lights go down on the scene.*)

SCENE 3

The lights come up on the jitney station early the following morning. It is obvious Youngblood has spent the night there. He sits on the couch figuring in his notebook. Turnbo enters.

TURNBO: You seen Becker this morning?

YOUNGBLOOD: He ain't come in yet.

TURNBO: You know his boy's getting out today?

YOUNGBLOOD: Yeah. Getting out of where?

TURNBO: You don't know about Becker's son?

YOUNGBLOOD: Know what?

TURNBO: Becker's boy been in the penitentiary for twenty years. He's getting out today.

YOUNGBLOOD: I ain't even knew Becker had a son.

TURNBO: Been in the penitentiary for twenty years! Right down there at the Western State Pen, and Becker ain't never been down there to see him once!

YOUNGBLOOD: Yeah?

TURNBO: I think it's a shame, Becker just wrote him off his list.

YOUNGBLOOD: Yeah. Well, that's his business, I guess.

TURNBO: Hell! That's his own son and if he ain't gonna stand by him, who's gonna? He ain't got nobody else. It killed his mama. Lucille ain't none of his mama. His mama died about a month after he went in. When the judge sentenced him to the electric chair, his mama just fell dead away. They brought her home and put her in the bed, and she laid right up there till she died.

YOUNGBLOOD: Gave him the electric chair?

TURNBO: That's right. Sure did. I was there! He later got it commuted to life.

YOUNGBLOOD: What he do to get the electric chair?

TURNBO: See, Becker's boy . . . Clarence is his name but everybody call him Booster . . . See now, Booster he liked that science. You know the science fair that they have over at the Buhl Planetarium every year where they have all them science experiments, where they make the water run uphill and things like that? Booster won first place three years in a row. He the only one who ever did that. I can't even count how many times he had his picture in the paper. They let him into the University of Pittsburgh. You know back then they didn't have too many colored out there, but they was trying to catch up to the Russians and they didn't care if he was colored or not. Gave him a scholarship and everything. Becker was just as proud as he could be. Him and Booster was always close. Becker used to take him hunting down around Wheeling, West Virginia. They go hunting and fishing. Becker didn't have but the one boy. After he was born the doctor told his wife that if she had another one it was liable to kill her. Say she was lucky to have the one. Anyway, Booster goes out to Pitt there and he meets this old white gal. Young gal . . . about eighteen she was. Of course Booster wasn't about nineteen himself. Now her old man was some kind of big shot down there at Gulf Oil. Had a lot of money and had done bought the gal a car for her birthday. Booster and that gal . . . they just go everywhere together. She ride him around like she was his chauffeur. Of course, she let him drive it too. I believe he drove it more than she did. That gal was crazy about Booster, and they was just sneaking around and sneaking around, you know. She didn't want her daddy to know she was fooling around with no colored boy. Well, one day, see, her father was up here in the neighborhood looking for one of them whores. He find one and she tell him to drive up the dead-end street there by the school, so she can turn the trick in the car. Don't you know they pulled right up in back of this gal's car where her and Booster done went to fool around! Her father recognizes the car and he goes over and looks inside and there's Booster just banging the hell out of his daughter! Well, that cracker went crazy. He just couldn't stand the sight of Booster screwing that gal and went to yanking open the car door. Booster didn't know who he was. All he knew was some crazy white man done opened the door and was screaming his head off. He proceeded to beat the man half to death. To get to the short of it . . . the police come and the gal said that she was driving downtown on her way home from a movie, and when she stopped for a red light, Booster jumped into her car and made her drive up there on the dead-end street . . . where he raped her. They arrested Booster and Becker got him out on bail 'cause he knew the gal was lying. The first day he was out . . . the first day! . . . he went over to that gal's house and shot her dead right on the front porch.

YOUNGBLOOD: Served the bitch right!

TURNBO: What you talking about! I knew you ain't had no sense. I don't know why I try and talk to you.

YOUNGBLOOD: Served her right for lying!

(The phone rings.)

TURNBO: That ain't no cause to kill nobody! I don't care if she was lying. See, that's what's wrong with you young folks. Don't take time to stop and think before you speak. "Serve the bitch right!" That's all you know.

YOUNGBLOOD: It does!

TURNBO: Fool! What is you talking about? That boy ain't had no right to kill that gal!

YOUNGBLOOD: She lied on him, didn't she?

TURNBO: That gal you got have a right to kill you 'cause you lyin' to her?

YOUNGBLOOD: We ain't talking about me. Stay out of my business!

TURNBO: Your business is already in the street. Everybody know how you misuse that gal, keeping her tied up in the house with that baby while you run around with her sister and don't give her two pennies to buy the baby no milk.

(Youngblood, enraged, rushes Turnbo and grabs him by the collar.)

YOUNGBLOOD: You stay the fuck out of my business!

TURNBO: Now you wanna beat me up for telling the truth. Well, go ahead, I'm an old man. Go ahead, it'll make you proud to hit an old man.

(Youngblood tries to restrain himself.)

YOUNGBLOOD: You stay out my business, Turnbo. I'm warning you!

TURNBO: I done told you your business is in the street.

(Youngblood loses control and punches Turnbo in the mouth. The blow knocks Turnbo to the floor and bloodies his mouth. Turnbo gets up and glares at Youngblood. Turnbo starts out the door just as Becker enters.)

YOUNGBLOOD: You just stay the fuck out of my business!

BECKER: What's going on? *(Notices Turnbo's bloody mouth)* What happened, Turnbo?

YOUNGBLOOD: You tell him to stay out of my business and everything will be straight. I don't get in his business and I don't want him in mine.

TURNBO: You know what I done already told you.

(*Youngblood tries to get to Turnbo, but Becker is in between the two of them.*)

BECKER: Hold it! Hold it! What's going on here?

(*Youngblood strains to get at Turnbo.*)

YOUNGBLOOD: This motherfucker . . . got his nose . . . all up in my business.

TURNBO: Let him go, Becker. I ain't scared of him. All I did was tell him where his business was. In the gutter!

(*Youngblood starts toward Turnbo. Becker grabs him. Youngblood struggles to get free.*)

YOUNGBLOOD: Let me go, Becker! Let me go!

BECKER: Hold it, Youngblood! There ain't gonna be no more fighting in here! Go on, Turnbo. I'll take care of him. You go on.

(*Turnbo exits.*)

What done got in you, boy. Hitting an old man like that. I can't have you fighting and causing trouble. You and Turnbo don't get along . . . just don't speak to him.

YOUNGBLOOD: I don't want him talking and speaking rumors about my business. That's all! That's all I want!

(*Turnbo, very excited, kicks open the door, drawing a pistol on Youngblood.*)

TURNBO: You don't believe your business is in the street! Is that right! Is that right!

BECKER: Turnbo!

TURNBO: Come on! You young punk! Come on! Hit me again! You don't believe that your business is in the street. I'll tell you something else. I done had that gal of yours.

YOUNGBLOOD: You lying motherfucker!

BECKER: Put that gun up, Turnbo!

TURNBO: Yeah. Come on! Jump at me! And I'll blow your ass to kingdom come!

YOUNGBLOOD: You lying motherfucker!

TURNBO: You think I'm lying, huh! I'll tell you how much I'm lying.

(Becker moves in between them.)

BECKER: Yeah, you lying. Why you wanna tell that boy that lie? That gal ain't give you the time of day.

TURNBO: Stay out of this, Becker!

BECKER: Don't lie to the boy like that. (Moving toward Turnbo) Come on now, put the gun up.

YOUNGBLOOD: Just because you used to them lowlife women don't mean everybody else is.

(Turnbo cocks back the hammer.)

TURNBO: You keep it up! You keep it up!

BECKER: You don't want to do that now; it ain't worth all that. Come on, Turnbo. The boy ain't meant nothing. He just young and foolish. I'll straighten him up. He just young. He don't know no better. Come on, put that gun up.

TURNBO: Boy, you got one more time to mess with me again! Just one more time!

(Turnbo puts the gun back in his pocket. Becker guides Turnbo to the door, and they exit together. Youngblood stands motionless in the middle of the room. Becker reenters.)

BECKER: Goddamn! If it ain't one thing it's another. Youngblood, you stay away from Turnbo! Just stay out of his way!

YOUNGBLOOD: I ain't studying him. That gun don't scare me.

BECKER: I ain't asked you was you studying him.

YOUNGBLOOD: When they made one gun they didn't stop making them.

BECKER: Just stay clear of him and don't say nothing to him. You can't go around hitting everybody that don't see eye to eye with you. Turnbo carry that gun in his car and if you push him far enough he'll run out there and get it. That ain't the first time. One of these days he's gonna use it. *(The phone rings)* So you just stay clear of him. The less words you have with Turnbo the better. *(Answering the phone)* Car service. *(Pause)* Where you going? *(Pause)* All right. Red Chevy.

(Fielding enters.)

FIELDING: Hey, Youngblood. Becker, what happened to Turnbo? He's sitting out there in his car cussing up a blue streak.

BECKER *(To Youngblood)*: 1845 Bedford. They're going to the bus station.

YOUNGBLOOD: I ain't carrying no suitcases in my car, Becker.

BECKER: You are if you want to jitney out of here.

(Fielding gets the drift of what is happening.)

FIELDING: What's the address? I'll make the trip.

BECKER: It's Youngblood's trip and he's gonna pull his weight around here.

YOUNGBLOOD: What you mean pull my weight? I pull my weight. I just don't want to mess up my car.

BECKER: How in the hell is putting somebody's suitcase in your trunk gonna mess up your car? That's what it's designed for! I done it for eighteen years and ain't never messed up my car. You talk like a fool.

FIELDING: Let me go, Becker.

YOUNGBLOOD: What's the address?

BECKER: 1845 Bedford.

(*Youngblood exits.*)

FIELDING: Why you wanna force that boy to haul things when he don't want to?

BECKER: Stay out of this, Fielding. It ain't none of your business.

FIELDING: I just asked 'cause I don't see much sense in it. If the boy don't want to haul people's things, he's got a right not to haul them, the way I see it. I ain't getting into nothing.

(*Turnbo enters.*)

TURNBO: Becker! You better straighten up that young fool before I be done killed him! I told you all along that boy ain't got no sense! Punching me in my mouth!

BECKER: I done talked to him, Turnbo.

FIELDING: Youngblood hit you? You all been fighting? What was you all fighting about?

TURNBO: He's got one more time! I'm telling you, Becker! Damn fool gonna hit me 'cause I tell him the truth. He is fooling around with that gal's sister and everybody knows it!

FIELDING: Who, Peaches?

TURNBO: I done seen him and her sister riding around here more than one time. He leave that gal at home to take care of the baby while he run around in the street with her sister. How many times you seen her come by here to try and track him down so she can get some money to buy that baby some milk? How many times you seen her?

(*Fielding opens a bottle and begins to drink.*)

FIELDING: Oh, I seen her by here before.

BECKER: Turnbo, you might come out better if you stayed out of people's business.

TURNBO: I ain't in nobody's business. We was having a conversation and it come up. I just speak my mind. I ain't never been one to bite my tongue about expressing an opinion and I ain't gonna start now. The only thing is, you better get that boy straightened out.

(Becker notices Fielding drinking.)

BECKER: Fielding! Goddamn it! I done told you about drinking in here!

FIELDING: I was just having a little nip, Becker.

BECKER: Well, that's it! I can't have you drinking and running jitneys out of here! That's it, your time is up! You done run you last jitney out of here!

FIELDING: What you talking about?

BECKER: You heard me. I know I speak clearly enough.

FIELDING *(Apologizing)*: I ain't done nothing. I just had a little nip.

BECKER: I told you time and again about drinking in the station. That's it! I ain't got no more conversation for you.

FIELDING: You see this, Turnbo?

BECKER *(To Turnbo)*: Fielding is out! I don't want him running no more trips out of here. I told him time and again about that drinking.

FIELDING: What is you talking about? *(The phone rings)* I paid my monthly dues and the month ain't up yet. I ain't going nowhere!

(Becker takes some money out of his pocket.)

BECKER: Here. Here's your money.

(Fielding doesn't take the money. Becker lays it down on top of the stove.)

There's your money. Take it and get out of here.

FIELDING: I ain't taking nothing. I paid for two more weeks, and two more weeks is what I get.

BECKER: There's your money. Now we straight. (*Answering the phone*) Car service. (*Pause*) 2719 Francis Street Projects? Be right there. Turnbo, take that trip.

(*Turnbo starts to exit.*)

FIELDING: That's my trip, Turnbo!

BECKER: I done told you, you ain't running no more trips out of this station. Take your money and get out.

FIELDING: Who the hell do you think you are? You ain't running over me, Becker!

BECKER: Take your money and get out. Go on, Turnbo.

TURNBO: I don't want to get in the middle of this. I don't want to be in nobody's business.

BECKER: I'll take it. (*To Fielding*) You just be gone when I get back. (*Exits*)

FIELDING (*Calling after Becker*): This is a free country! I'm a free man! You can't tell me what to do! This is the United States of America. (*Takes another drink*) You see that, Turnbo? You see that?

(*The lights fade to black.*)

SCENE 4

The lights come up on the jitney station a half hour later. Turnbo and Fielding have been joined by Booster, who stands looking out the window. He is dressed in his prison-issued suit, and wears a white shirt without a tie.

FIELDING: Yeah, I know your daddy real good. I've been driving jitneys with him for eight years now. And I worked off and on with him when he was down at the mill too. That's when I was younger. Here, get yourself a nip.

(Fielding drinks from the bottle and offers it to Booster, who declines.)

BOOSTER: No thanks. You say he should be back in a minute?

TURNBO: He just went out on a short trip. He'll be back in no time. Things done changed since the last time you seen them, I reckon.

BOOSTER: Yeah, pretty much.

TURNBO: They're tearing everything down around here. All along Wylie there. You see they done tore everything down. They gonna tear this building down. They gonna board it up first of the month. We're gonna have to move. Either that or split up. We can't stay here no more.

FIELDING: You got to have somebody you can count on you know. Now my wife . . . we been separated for twenty-two years now . . . but I ain't never loved nobody the way I loved that woman. You know what I mean?

BOOSTER: Yeah, I know.

FIELDING: She the only thing in the world that I got. I had a dream once. It just touched me so. I was climbing this ladder. It was a solid gold ladder and I was climbing up into heaven. I get to the top of the ladder and I can see all the saints sitting around . . . and I could see her too . . . sitting there in her place in glory. Just as I reached the top my hand started to slip and I called out for help. All them saints and angels . . . Saint Peter and everybody . . . they just sat there and looked at me. She was the only one who left her seat in glory and tried to help me to keep from falling back down that ladder. I ain't never forgot that. When I woke up . . . tears was all over my face, just running all down in my ears and I laid there and cried like a baby . . . 'cause that meant so much to me. To find out after all these years, that she still loved me.

BOOSTER: That's some heavy drama, my man.

FIELDING: Oh, she love me all right. I know she do. I ain't seen that woman in twenty-two years . . . but I know she loves me.

(Fielding takes another drink as Becker enters. He stands in the doorway glaring at Fielding.)

Hey, Becker. I was just talking to your son.

BECKER: I thought I told you not to be here when I got back.

(Fielding staggers to his feet.)

FIELDING: All right, Becker. You win. I'm gone.

(Fielding starts toward the door. Becker crosses to the stove and picks up the money.)

BECKER: Here. Take your money with you.

(Fielding takes the money and starts to exit. He stops.)

FIELDING: Let me work the two weeks. I'll be sober in the morning. It's almost over, Becker. It's almost over.

BECKER: Go on home, Fielding. I'll see you tomorrow. You be sober when you come in here.

(Fielding starts to exit. Becker holds out his hand for the money. Fielding gives it to him and exits. Becker turns to face Booster.)

BOOSTER: How you doing, Pop?

(Booster holds out his hand. Becker takes it awkwardly.)

BECKER: Fine. Fine. How you doing? You look good.

BOOSTER: I feel pretty good. Lucille told me you'd be down here.

BECKER: Turnbo, go next door and tell Clifford to send me one of them fish sandwiches, will you?

(Turnbo exits reluctantly.)

So you doing all right, huh?

BOOSTER: I don't know. I been looking around. I don't know what to think. People going everywhere. All up and down. Dogs and cats. Airplanes. It's gonna take me a while to get used to things.

BECKER: So what you gonna do with the rest of your life now that you done ruined it?

BOOSTER: Hey Pop . . . I just stopped by to say hi. See how you doing.

BECKER: Can't get no job. Who's gonna hire you? You got a mark on you a foot wide. They can see you coming. You just took your life and threw it away like it wasn't worth nothing.

BOOSTER: I don't want all this. I don't want to hear about my life being ruined. I just stopped by to say hi. I don't want this. I done paid my debt.

BECKER: You don't even know where your debt begins.

BOOSTER: I know where it ended. It ended after I did them twenty years. I don't owe nobody nothing. They tried to give me that parole five years ago and I turned it down because I didn't want to owe nobody nothing. I didn't want nobody looking after me telling me what to do . . . asking me questions about my life. I walk in here to say hi and you start telling me my life is ruined. How I'm gonna get a job . . . I don't want that, Pop. I'm a grown man. I'm thirty-nine years old. I'm young. I'm healthy. I ain't got no complaints . . . and I don't carry no grudges. Whatever was between us these twenty years I put aside. I don't hold no grudge.

BECKER: Who the hell care what you hold? I'm the one got to walk around here with people pointing at me. Talking about me behind my back. "There go his father. That's him." People trying to sneak a look at me out the corner of their eye. See if they can see something wrong with me. If they can see what kind of man would raise a boy to do something like that. You done marked me and you walk in here talking about you ain't got no grudge!

BOOSTER: I'm just saying I don't have no hard feeling that you didn't come to see me, Pop. I been thinking about my life and all the things you did for me . . . all the things you gave me . . . all the things you taught me. All the things—

BECKER: Everything I give you . . . you threw away. You ain't got nothing now. You got less than the day you was born. Then you had some dignity. Some innocence . . . You ain't got nothing now. You took and you threw it all away. You thirty-nine years old and you ain't got nothing.

BOOSTER: Naw Pop, you wrong. I may have lost some things. I may have missed some things . . . but that don't mean I ain't got nothing.

BECKER: You ain't got nothing, boy!

BOOSTER: Well, since we talking about what we got . . . what you got, Pop? You the boss of a jitney station.

BECKER: I am the boss of a jitney station. I'm a deacon down at the church. Got me a little house. It ain't much but it's mine. I worked twenty-seven years at the mill . . . got me a pension. I got a wife. I got respect. I can walk anywhere and hold my head up high. What I ain't got is a son that did me honor . . . The Bible say, "Honor thy father and thy mother." I ain't got that. I ain't got a son I can be proud of. That's what I ain't got. A son to come up behind me . . . living a good honest decent life. I got a son who people point to and say, "That's Becker's boy. That's the one that killed that gal. That's Becker's boy. The one they gave the electric chair. That's Becker's boy."

BOOSTER: I did what I had to do and I paid for it.

BECKER: What you had to do! What you had to do! What law is there say you have to kill somebody if they tell a lie on you? Where does it say that? If somebody tell a lie on you, you have to kill them? Who taught you that? It was a lie! The gal told a lie! If it was the truth then go ahead and kill yourself. Go on and throw your life away. But it was a lie!

We could have fought the lie. I'd already lined up a lawyer . . . together we could have fought the lie.

BOOSTER: A lawyer wasn't gonna make no difference. I wasn't going to the penitentiary for nothing. I wasn't gonna live a lie.

BECKER: I taught you two wrongs don't make a right.

BOOSTER: Sometime they do. Sometime you got to add it up that way. Otherwise it's just one wrong after another and you never get to what's right. I wasn't gonna hang no sign around my neck say rapist.

BECKER: You gonna hang one say murderer? That's better?

BOOSTER: That's honest.

BECKER: That gal lying didn't make you wrong in the world. A lie don't make you wrong in the world.

BOOSTER: It don't make you right either. Right is right and right don't wrong nobody. You taught me that.

BECKER: I taught you to respect life. I taught you all of life is precious.

BOOSTER: Yeah Pop, you taught me a lot of things. And a lot of things I had to learn on my own. Like that time Mr. Rand came to the house to collect the rent when we was two months behind. I don't remember what year it was. I just know it was winter. Grandma Ada had just died and you got behind in the rent 'cause you had to help pay for her funeral.

I don't know if you knew it, Pop, but you were a big man. Everywhere you went people treated you like a big man. You used to take me to the barbershop with you. You'd walk in there and fill up the whole place. Everybody would stop cussing because Jim Becker had walked in. I would just look at you and wonder how you could be that big. I wanted to be like that. I would go to school and try to make myself feel big. But I never could. I told myself that's okay . . . when I get grown I'm gonna be big like that. Walk into the barbershop and have everybody stop and look at me.

That day when Mr. Rand came to the house it was snowing. You came out on the porch and he started shouting and cussing and threatening to put us out in the street where we belonged. I was waiting for you to tell him to shut up . . . to get off your porch. But you just looked at him and promised you would have the money next month. Mama came to the door and Mr. Rand kept shouting and cussing. I looked at Mama . . . she was trying to get me to go in the house . . . and I looked at you . . . and you had got smaller. The longer he shouted the smaller you got. When we went back to the barbershop you didn't seem so big no more. You was the same size as everybody else. You was just another man in the barbershop. That's when I told myself if I ever got big I wouldn't let nothing make me small.

Then when I met Susan McKnight and found out her daddy was the vice-president of Gulf Oil . . . that's when I got big. That made me a big man. I felt like I was somebody. I felt like I could walk in the barbershop and fill it up the way you did. Then when she told that lie on me that's when I woke up. That's when I realized that I wasn't big from the inside. I wasn't big on my own. When she told that lie it made me small. I wanted to do something that said I wasn't just another nigger . . . that I was Clarence Becker. I wanted to make them remember my name. And I thought about you standing there and getting small and Mr. Rand shouting and Susan McKnight shouting out that lie and I realized it was my chance to make the Beckers big again . . . my chance to show what I had learned on my own. I thought you would understand. I thought you would be proud of me.

BECKER: Proud of you for killing somebody!

BOOSTER: No, Pop. For being a warrior. For dealing with the world in ways that you didn't or couldn't or wouldn't.

BECKER: Boy, you trying to say I had something to do with you pulling that trigger. You trying to say that it's all my fault because I didn't knock Mr. Rand on his ass so I could keep a roof over your head. So you wouldn't have to sleep in the street, in the cold and the snow.

BOOSTER: No, Pop. I did it.

BECKER: You gonna knock Mr. Rand on his ass for me by killing that gal.

BOOSTER: No, Pop. It was for me. I did it for myself. But it didn't add up the way I thought it would. I was wrong. I can see that now.

BECKER: You could have been something. You had every advantage . . . I tried to fix it so you didn't have to follow up behind me . . . So you could go on and go further. So you could have a better life. I did without so you could have.

BOOSTER: Hey Pop, you took your road . . . you made your choices, you done what was right for you. I made my choice. I took my road and I did what was right for me. I paid the consequences. Now that's over and done. Let's just say I stopped by to say hi and leave it at that. (Starts to exit)

BECKER: You want to know why I never came to see you?

BOOSTER: No, I don't want to know. That's your business.

BECKER: I kept seeing your face at your mother's funeral. How you just stood there and never shed a tear. Stood there with a scowl on your face. And now you want to come in here and ridicule me 'cause I didn't knock Mr. Rand on his ass. You wanna know why? I'll tell you why. Because I had your black ass crying to be fed. Crying to have a roof over your head. To have clothes to wear to school and lunch money in your pocket. That's why! Because I had a family. I had responsibility. If I had knocked him on his ass you would have went hungry. You wouldn't have had clothes on your back or a roof over your head. I done what I had to do. I swallowed my pride and let them mess over me, all the time saying, "You bastards got it coming. Look out! Becker's boy's coming to straighten this shit out! You're not gonna fuck over him! He's gonna grow big and strong!

Watch out for Becker's boy! Becker's taking this ass-whipping so his boy can stride through this shit like Daniel in the lion's den! Watch out for Becker's boy!" (*He has worked himself into a frenzy and is now near tears*) And what I get, huh? You tell me. What I get? Tell me what I get! Tell me! What I get? What I get, huh?

(*Booster moves toward him.*)

BOOSTER: Pop . . .

BECKER: Stay away from me! What I get, huh? What I get? Tell me?

(*Booster is silent.*)

I get a murderer, that's what. A murderer.

BOOSTER: Pop, look . . .

BECKER: And the way your mama loved you. You killed her! You know that? You a double murderer!

BOOSTER: I ain't killed her, Pop. You know that.

BECKER: What you call it? That woman took sick the day that judge sentenced you and she ain't never walked or said another word or ate another thing for twenty-three days. She just laid up in that room until she died. Now you tell me that ain't killing her. Tell me that ain't killing her!

BOOSTER: Every day Mama came to that courtroom by herself. Where was you? Anybody could see how it was wearing her down. Where was you when she needed somebody to hold her hand . . . when she needed a shoulder to cry on . . . somebody to talk to? Where was you . . . not for me . . . but for her . . . the woman you loved? When she fainted in that courtroom I tried to get to her . . . but I had six deputies holding me back. What was holding you? Where was you them twenty-three days when she was dying?

45

BECKER: I was trying to keep her alive. Trying to get her to eat something . . . trying to get her—

BOOSTER: It wasn't about eating, Pop. That's not what she needed . . . a bowl of soup. She needed to know that you were there for her. That you would be there for her when she got up. That she could count on you to support her. But you turned your back. Clinging to your rules . . .

BECKER: Don't you say nothing to me about turning my back!

BOOSTER: What you call it?

BECKER: I was there! I was holding her hand when she died. Where were you? Locked up in a cage like some animal. That's what killed her. To hear the judge say that the life she brought in the world was unfit to live. That you be "remanded to the custody of the Commissioner of Corrections at Western State Penitentiary and there to be executed in the electric chair. This order to be carried out thirty days from today." Ain't that what the judge said? Ain't that what she heard? "This order to be carried out thirty days from today." That's what killed her. She didn't want to live them thirty days. She didn't want to be alive to hear on the eleven o'clock news that they had killed you. So don't you say nothing to me about turning my back when I nursed that woman, talked to her, held her hand, prayed over her and the last words to come out of her mouth was your name. I was there! Where were you, Mr. Murderer? Mr. Unfit to Live Amongst Society. Where were you when your mama was dying and calling your name? (*Stops, taking a moment to gather himself*) You are my son. I helped to bring you into this world. But from this moment on . . . I'm calling the deal off. You ain't nothing to me, boy. You just another nigger on the street.

(*Becker exits. Booster stands looking down at the floor. The phone rings. The lights fade to black.*)

ACT TWO

The lights come up on the jitney station. It is the next day. Doub sits in one of the chairs reading a newspaper. Turnbo looks at a magazine.

TURNBO: Now here's another something I don't understand. Lena Horne. How come everybody say she pretty? I even hear some people say she's the prettiest woman in the world.

DOUB: I ain't gonna say all that. But if she ain't, she right up there.

TURNBO: She ain't as pretty as Sarah Vaughan.

DOUB: Naw. Naw. We talking about Lena Horne. Some things just ain't open to debate. Lena Horne being pretty is one of them.

TURNBO: Sarah Vaughan got more nature than Lena Horne.

DOUB: What's that supposed to mean? Even if she do . . . how you gonna measure it? It ain't like saying she got more hair or something.

TURNBO: She got a prettier smile too. A lot of people sleeping on Sarah Vaughan.

47

DOUB: How you know how many people sleeping with her?

TURNBO: I said sleeping on her, not with her. Everybody talking about Lena Horne and people sleeping on Sarah Vaughan. People don't know Sarah Vaughan got more of everything than Lena Horne. They just believe what they hear. But Sarah Vaughan got more nature . . . got a prettier smile . . . got more personality . . . and she can sing better.

DOUB: We ain't said nothing about that. We ain't said nothing about singing. You said Lena Horne wasn't pretty.

TURNBO: She ain't. She ain't as pretty as people think. People just think she's pretty.

DOUB: Oh, I see . . . people just think dogs bite. People just think if you cut yourself you'll bleed.

(Fielding enters.)

Hey Fielding . . . Turnbo say Lena Horne ain't pretty.

FIELDING: Some people say shit don't stink. Sooner or later they gonna find out otherwise. It's them pretty women like Lena Horne get a man killed.

TURNBO: You ain't got to be pretty to get a man killed. Any woman will get a man killed if he ain't careful. Am I right, Doub?

DOUB: You right. That's why I don't talk about women. I don't talk about money either. Them is the two things you never hear me talk about too much. Them is the two things that get most people killed.

FIELDING: Women and money will get a preacher killed.

DOUB: I seen it happen. You go and ask one of them fellows say, "Why you do that?" You have to catch him after he cooled down. You have to get him down there in jail after about six or nine months and you ask him why he killed so and so. And he'll tell you. He'll tell you he had a woman stay on his mind and he couldn't think right. Then when he seen somebody else talking to her seem like they was the cause of all his trouble . . . wasn't nothing left to do but kill him. That's why if you see me talking to a woman you can bet it's my sister or my aunt.

TURNBO: You right. The first thing a man do when he get a woman he don't want nobody else to have her. He say this is mine. I'm gonna hold on to this. I'm gonna go over and see Betty Jean but I'm gonna hold on to this. If I catch anybody sneaking around her sniffing . . . I'm gonna bust his nose and break both of his legs . . . if I don't shoot him with my forty-four. He say that and then he go on over to Betty Jean. He don't know some fellow done said the same thing about catching somebody around Betty Jean. That fellow . . . he go over to see Betty Sue while this other fellow sniffing around his Betty Jean. Sooner or later . . . somebody gonna get their wires crossed. Somebody gonna see Betty Jean when he should have been seeing Betty Sue and that'll be all she wrote for him. The only thing left to do is write it on his tombstone. "Here lie Bubba Boo. Was caught with Betty Jean instead of Betty Sue."

DOUB: They got that on a whole lot of tombstones.

(The phone rings.)

FIELDING (Answering the phone): Car service. (Pause) Yeah, sure I'll tell him. Turnbo, that was Aunt Lil. She say you supposed to pick her up at the doctor's.

TURNBO (Exasperated): You know she done joined the Jehovah Witness. When I come back I'll be able to tell you anything you wanna know about the Bible. (Exits)

(The phone rings.)

FIELDING (Answering the phone): Car service. (Pause) Yeah, I'll be right there. Green car.

DOUB: No, wait a minute. I thought Becker put you out.

FIELDING: Aw, me and Becker straight. (*Exits*)

(*Youngblood enters carrying tools.*)

YOUNGBLOOD: I cleaned the flywheel and replaced the belt. Another ten thousand miles and you gonna need a new alternator.

DOUB: Thanks.

YOUNGBLOOD: Hey Doub, what's this I hear about the station closing?

DOUB: You just now finding out? They fixing to board up the whole block. Tear it down and build some houses.

YOUNGBLOOD: Damn! What they wanna do that for?

DOUB: I'm glad to see them do it. It's about time they done something around here. They been talking for years about how they was gonna fix it up.

YOUNGBLOOD: White folks ain't got no sense of timing. They wait till I get in the position to buy me a house and then they pull the rug out from under me!

DOUB: That white man ain't paying you no mind. You ought to stop thinking like that. They been planning to tear these shacks down before you was born. You keep thinking everybody's against you and you ain't never gonna get nothing. I seen a hundred niggers too lazy to get up out the bed in the morning, talking about the white man is against them. That's just an excuse. You want to make something of your life, then the opportunity is there. You just have to shake off that "white folks is against me" attitude. Hell, they don't even know you alive.

YOUNGBLOOD: They knew I was alive when they drafted me and sent me over to Vietnam to be shot at. They knew I was alive then!

DOUB: You ain't the only one they sent. They sent a whole lot of other folks too. Some of them wasn't lucky enough to make it back alive. You ain't the only one been in the Army.

I went into the Army in 1950. Looking to make something of myself. That was after the war. I didn't know they was gonna pull out a map, stick a pin in it and say, "Let's go kill some people over here." I wasn't in the Army but four months and they had me in Korea. Second Division. Company B. Fourth Battalion. It was a detail company. I think at that time the only dead body I had seen was my grandmama when Foster buried her. That's all I knew about a dead body. But I was meant to find out quick. The third day they put us on some trucks and drove out to the front lines. I was scared as I could get. The last words I remember my mama saying to me was how she was praying I didn't get sent to the front lines. I wasn't in Korea but three days and here I was on the front lines. Got out there and everything was quiet. The sergeant told us to get down off the trucks. We got down and started walking. Got near about two hundred yards when we saw our first body. Then another one. Then three more. The sergeants say, "All right boys, we gonna clean up. I want you to stack the bodies six high." I never will forget that. "I want you to stack the bodies six high." Not five. Not seven. Six high. And that's what I did for the next nine months. Clean up the battlefield. It took me six months before I got to where I could keep my supper down. After that it didn't bother me no more. Never did learn how to do nothing else. They was supposed to teach me but they never did. They just never paid me no mind. There was a whole bunch of us they never paid no mind. What I'm trying to tell you is the white man ain't got no personal war against you 'cause you buying a house and they gonna tear down this block. You too young to be depending on driving jitneys. Is that what you want to do all your life?

YOUNGBLOOD: Naw, but where else am I gonna make fifty dollars a day tax-free? Where else am I gonna get the advantage of not paying taxes?

DOUB: How old are you? Twenty-four? Why don't you go to school under the GI Bill? Become something. Make something of your life. You can be anything you want. Be a pilot or a engineer or something. Like I tell my boys, the world's opened up to you. When I was your age, the only thing you could get a job doing was busing dishes, running elevators and cleaning out toilets. Things like that. It ain't like that now. You can be anything you want. You're young, act kinda crazy, but you got some sense. You don't waste your money. You got sense enough to buy a house. Go on to school, Youngblood. You too young to be counting on driving jitneys.

YOUNGBLOOD: I'm worried about right now. How I'm gonna get me some furniture and pay that three-hundred-dollar-a-month mortgage.

DOUB: Why don't you try to get on with another station?

YOUNGBLOOD: They all filled up. If Ace hadn't died I wouldn't even have got on here.

DOUB: Talk to Becker. See if he can get you on down at the mill. He got some pull down there.

YOUNGBLOOD: I don't want to work in no mill. I done seen what the mills do to people and I swore I'd never work in no mill. The mills suck all the life out of you. That's not for me. I don't want that. I'll do anything but I don't want that.

(*The phone rings.*)

DOUB: It ain't all the time what you want. Sometime it's what you need. Black folks always get the two confused. (*Answering the phone*) Car service. (*Pause*) Naw, he ain't here right now. I'll tell him. (*Hangs up the phone*) Somebody named Glucker from J&L Steel wants Becker to call him back.

YOUNGBLOOD: Hey Doub, what you gonna do when the station close?

DOUB: I don't know. Becker talking about quitting. I wanted to get together and see if we can find a place to move the station. If that don't work, I guess I'll just run the bus line till something else comes up. I ain't too worried. I got my railroad pension, and I ain't got nobody but myself, so I'll be all right.

(Fielding enters.)

FIELDING: Hey, Doub. Youngblood. We ain't got but two more weeks, huh?

DOUB: Yeah, that's right. They gonna board it up first of the month.

FIELDING: What you gonna do?

DOUB: I don't know, Fielding.

FIELDING: Well, it's a shame. That's all I got to say about it. You see Becker's boy yesterday?

DOUB: Naw, I ain't seen him. Did he come by here?

FIELDING: Oh, yeah, he come by. Me and Turnbo was here. Good-looking boy. He come by to see his daddy. Big, strong boy. Youngblood, you and Turnbo get straightened out?

YOUNGBLOOD: We okay. As long as he stay out my business.

FIELDING: You all ain't gonna be okay long. Turnbo's just like that. He get in everybody's business. You can't pay him no mind. You got to ignore what he say.

DOUB: What . . . you and Turnbo had some words?

FIELDING: Turnbo pulled a gun on him.

DOUB: He did what?

FIELDING: Pulled a gun on him.

DOUB: That nigger's crazy. He's gonna kill somebody one of these days with that damn gun. Either that or somebody's gonna kill him. That makes the fourth or fifth time he done pulled that gun on somebody. One time he pulled that gun on a man for fifty cents. Man took a trip and told him he'd pay him later. Turnbo seen the man sitting next door eating breakfast. He went in there . . . kicked open the door . . . waving that gun around. Talking about killing somebody over fifty cents. The man ain't had a penny. He done talked the waitress into letting him owe her too, and Turnbo wanna go in there and shoot the man. Somebody had to give him fifty cents to keep him from getting killed. You mark my words. One of these times he's gonna end up killing somebody.

(*Turnbo enters and everyone falls silent as they look at him.*)

TURNBO: You all want me to go back out so you can finish.

DOUB: I don't care what you do.

TURNBO: You all got quiet . . . like you was talking about me.

FIELDING: Naw, we wasn't . . .

DOUB: Yeah, we was talking about you. We was talking about how you gonna pull that gun on the wrong person one of these days.

TURNBO: You ain't got nothing to do with that, Doub. I ain't gonna let nobody take advantage of me, that's all, and that boy ain't got but one more time.

DOUB: Yeah, you right. I ain't got nothing to do with it. Let me shut up. (*Crosses to the door*) Youngblood, if you see Becker don't forget to tell him that Glucker from the mill called. (*Exits*)

FIELDING: Somebody called Becker from the mill?

TURNBO: Must be about Shealy's nephew. That boy broke into Taylor's with old man Pitt's son. Becker's trying to get him a job at the mill.

FIELDING: Oh, well he can do that. He's got a lot of pull down there. He done got a whole lot of people jobs. What you gonna do Turnbo when the station close down?

TURNBO: Oh, I'm set. I talked to Lewellen down on Centre. I'm gonna take Jim Bono's place. Bono's in the hospital with cancer.

FIELDING: No kidding. That's a shame.

TURNBO: What you gonna do?

FIELDING: I don't know. Doub say something about finding another place. I'm gonna wait and see what Becker say.

TURNBO: What about you, Youngblood?

YOUNGBLOOD: I ain't got nothing to say to you.

TURNBO: If that's the way you want it.

YOUNGBLOOD: You just stay clear of me, old man. Next time you gonna get hurt for real.

TURNBO: I ain't gonna let nobody do nothing to me.

FIELDING: Don't you all start now. Come on and be friends.

TURNBO: I ain't started nothing. I tried to talk to the man, willing to let bygones be bygones and he wanna threaten me.

(The phone rings.)

YOUNGBLOOD: I done said all I got to say to you.

TURNBO: Well all right then. If that's the way you want it. Good! *(Answering the phone)* Car service. *(Pause)* Fielding. *(Hands Fielding the phone)*

FIELDING: Hello? Oh, hi, Miss Mayberry. *(Pause)* Sure, I'll take you shopping. Are you ready now? *(Pause)* I'll be right there.

(Fielding bumps into Shealy as he exits. Shealy is dressed up.)

SHEALY: Did I get any calls this morning?

YOUNGBLOOD: Not that I know.

SHEALY: That gal say she was gonna call me at ten o'clock. I knew she was lying when she said it. Becker been here yet?

TURNBO: I ain't seen him. I hear Becker's upset about you using the phone to take numbers.

SHEALY: Becker's always upset about something.

(The phone rings. Booster enters.)

TURNBO (*Answering the phone*): Car service. Shealy. (*Hands the phone to Shealy*)

BOOSTER: Hey fellows. My old man been around here?

TURNBO: I ain't seen him all day. I just got here though. Young-blood, Becker been by at all?

YOUNGBLOOD: I ain't seen him.

SHEALY (*Into the phone*): Yeah. Three forty-seven . . .

TURNBO: He should be back in a minute.

SHEALY: . . . and six seventeen boxed for fifty cents . . . nine twenty-nine straight for a dollar. (*Takes out his pad and writes*) Yeah. Okay. (*Hangs up the phone*)

BOOSTER: You take numbers?

TURNBO: Yeah. Shealy, this is Becker's son. That's Shealy. He the number man.

BOOSTER: Give me three dollars on three nineteen, straight.

(*Shealy writes the number and gives Booster his slip.*)

If you all see my old man, tell him I was by to see him. (*Exits*)

YOUNGBLOOD: Shealy, I'm going next door to clean up. If Becker comes, tell him I got a message for him.

SHEALY: I ain't gonna be hanging around here all day. I'm gonna give that gal five more minutes.

TURNBO: Go on, I'll tell him.

YOUNGBLOOD: That's all right, I'll be right back. (*Exits*)

TURNBO: That boy ain't got good sense.

SHEALY: I hear you all had a go at it.

TURNBO: He's a damn fool. (*The phone rings. Answering it*) Car service. (*Pause*) Shealy.

SHEALY: Shealy. (*Pause*) Hey baby! (*Pause*) Sure. That's what I told you. Where you at? (*Pause*) Don't move. Stay right there. I'll be there in five minutes. (*Hangs up the phone*) Come on, Turnbo. Give me a ride down to the Ellis Hotel. This might be the one! If I don't see Rosie's face, I'll give you five dollars for the trip!

(The phone rings. Turnbo and Shealy exit. Youngblood enters carrying a cup of coffee. He takes out his book and begins to figure in it. Rena enters.)

YOUNGBLOOD: What you want around here?

RENA: I want to see you. You didn't come home last night.

YOUNGBLOOD: That's right. What for? You tell me, huh? What I'm gonna come home for? Being as how you might not be there.

RENA: Where did you go?

YOUNGBLOOD: What you care about where I went? I stayed here, if you got to know. I slept on the couch. What I'm gonna come home for with you making all them stupid accusations?

RENA: I ain't made no accusations. I just said I knew about you and Peaches.

YOUNGBLOOD: Somebody tell you they seen your sister in my car and you jump to conclusions. You don't know what I'm doing.

RENA: You right. I don't know what you doing. That's what I'm saying. It ain't like you ain't got no track record. If I remember correctly, you was leading the parade.

YOUNGBLOOD: I'm here. That should be enough. If I didn't want to be here I'd be somewhere else. Why can't you just take that?

RENA: Because it's not enough. I don't want somebody that think just 'cause they there, that's enough . . . they don't have to do nothing else. I want somebody who's gonna share with me . . . not hide things from me.

YOUNGBLOOD: You want to know what I was hiding from you? I'll tell you. I been hustling . . . working day and night . . . while you accuse me of running the streets . . . and all I'm trying to do is save enough money so I can buy a house so you and Jesse have someplace decent to live. I asked Peaches if she would go with me to look at houses, 'cause

I wanted to surprise you. I wanted to pull a truck up to the house and say, "Come on, baby, we moving." And drive on out to Penn Hills and pull that truck up in front of one of them houses and say, "This is yours. This is your house, baby." That's what she was trying to hide from you. That's why Turnbo seen her riding in my car all the time. I found a house and I come up a hundred and fifty dollars short from closing the deal, and I come and took the eighty dollars out the drawer.

RENA: A house? A house, Darnell? You bought a house without me!

YOUNGBLOOD: I wanted to surprise you.

RENA: You gonna surprise me with a house? Don't do that. A new TV maybe. A stereo . . . a couch . . . a refrigerator . . . okay. But don't surprise me with a house that I didn't even have a chance to pick out! That's what you been doing? That's the debt you had to pay?

YOUNGBLOOD: You always saying you don't want to live your whole life in the projects.

RENA: Darnell, you ain't bought no house without me. How many times in your life do you get to pick out a house?

YOUNGBLOOD: Wait till you see it. It's real nice. It's all on one floor . . . it's got a basement . . . like a little den. We can put the TV down there. I told myself Rena's gonna like this. Wait till she see I bought her a house.

RENA: Naw, you bought a den for Darnell . . . that's what you did. So you can sit down there and watch your football games. But what about the kitchen? The bathroom? How many windows does it have in the bedroom? Is there someplace for Jesse to play? How much closet space does it have? You can't just surprise me with a house and I'm supposed to say, "Oh, Darnell, that's nice." At one time I would have. But I'm not seventeen no more. I have responsibilities. I want to know if it has a hookup for a washer and dryer 'cause I got to wash Jesse's clothes.

I want to know if it has a yard and do it have a fence and how far Jesse has to go to school. I ain't thinking about where to put the TV. That's not what's important to me. And you supposed to know, Darnell. You supposed to know what's important to me like I'm supposed to know what's important to you. I'm not asking you to do it by yourself. I'm here with you. We in this together. See . . . house or no house we still ain't got the food money. But if you had come and told me . . . if you had shared that with me . . . we could have went to my mother and we could have got eighty dollars for the house and still had money for food. You just did it all wrong, Darnell. I mean, you did the right thing but you did it wrong.

YOUNGBLOOD: No matter what I do it's gonna come out wrong with you. That's why you jump to conclusions. That's why you accused me of running around with Peaches. You can't look and see that I quit going to parties all the time . . . that I quit running with Ba Bra and Earl . . . that I quit chasing women. You just look at me and see the old Darnell. If you can't change the way you look at me . . . then I may as well surrender now. I can't beat your memory of who I was if you can't see I've changed. I go out here and work like a dog to try and do something nice for you and no matter what I do, I can't never do it right 'cause all you see is the way I used to be. You don't see the new Darnell. You don't see I've changed.

RENA: I know people change . . . but I know they can slip back too.

YOUNGBLOOD: No, Rena . . . people believe what they want to believe . . . what they set up in their mind to believe. I know what it looked like when I was gone all the time and not bringing home any money. But you could have noticed that I was tired . . . you could have said, "Darnell ain't talking too much 'cause he's tired." You could have noticed that I didn't act like somebody running the streets

. . . that I didn't come home smelling like alcohol and perfume . . . that I didn't dress like somebody running the streets. If you had thought it all the way through, you could have noticed how excited I was when I got the UPS job . . . how I asked you if I could take it . . . you would have noticed how I was planning things . . . that I wasn't sitting around drinking beer and playing cards . . . how I would get up early on Sunday and go out to the airport to try to make a few extra dollars before the jitney station opened. But you ain't seen all that. You ain't seen the new Darnell. You still working off your memory. But the past is over and done with. I'm thinking about the future. You not the only one who thinks about Jesse. That's why I'm trying to do something different. That's why I'm trying to buy a house. Maybe I should have told you about the house. Maybe I did do it wrong. But I done it. I tried to show you I loved you, but what I get for it?

RENA: Okay, Darnell . . . you right. I could have seen all that. But what you ain't looking at is I changed too. We are both different people than we were . . . than when we first fell in love. I still love you, Darnell. But love can only go so far. When we were in high school that was enough. That was the world. That was everything. But it ain't everything no more. I don't have all the answers . . . sometimes I don't even have the right questions, but I do know it takes two to find them. All I know is we got somebody, a little two-year-old boy, counting on us.

YOUNGBLOOD: But I know when you place your hand in mine you got to say, "Darnell's not gonna let me down . . . he loves me." I don't want to make no more mistakes in life. I don't want to do nothing to mess this up. I don't want to get old and be talking about I had me this little old gal one time . . . but I ain't seen her in twenty-two years.

RENA: If that's not what you want then you got to let me know, Darnell. If we don't know what's important to one another and learn to share that then we can't make it. We can't make it with each other.

YOUNGBLOOD: I want you, baby . . . I told you that. You already my pride. I want you to be my joy. 'Cause there ain't but one thing I done wrong . . . stay away from you one night too long.

(They kiss for a long moment.)

RENA: Where's this house at?

YOUNGBLOOD: Penn Hills. It's got a nice kitchen too. Got a little yard. Got a nice bedroom. Got a real nice bedroom.

RENA: Oh, yeah. I can't wait to see it.

YOUNGBLOOD: Where's my boy?

RENA: At my mother's house. I got to go to my accounting class.

YOUNGBLOOD: You wanna ride?

RENA: I'll walk. I need the exercise.

YOUNGBLOOD: Naw, I'll give you a ride. I don't want to let you out of my sight. Matter of fact you might have to miss that accounting class.

RENA: What? You got something to teach me?

(They kiss again as Becker enters.)

BECKER: Hey . . . Hey . . . You all got to take that home.

RENA: How you doing, Mr. Becker?

BECKER: Oh, I'm all right. How you all doing?

YOUNGBLOOD: Well, Becker . . . I done bought me a house.

BECKER: Oh, yeah. Where'd you buy it at?

YOUNGBLOOD: Penn Hills.

BECKER: Good! They got some nice houses out there. That's a smart move, Youngblood. I'm glad to see you do it. Ain't nothing like owning some property. They might even call you for jury duty. Most young men be on the other side of the law. How old is the baby now?

RENA: Two. He look like he's three. Big as he is.

BECKER: Ain't nothing left to do now but to get married. Come November it'll be seventeen years that me and Lucille been together. Seventeen years. I told her say, "Work with me." She say okay. I wasn't sure what it meant myself. I thought it meant pull or push together. But she showed me one can push and the other can pull . . . as long as it's in the same direction. You know what I mean? It ain't all gonna flow together all the time. That's life. As long as it don't break apart. When you look around you'll see that all you got is each other. There ain't much more. Even when it look like there is . . . you come one day to find out there ain't much more worth having. Now I ain't getting in your business or nothing, Youngblood, but the next time you feel like you want to spend the night apart . . . do like I do . . . go sleep on the couch in the living room. Don't put your business in the street. You put your business in the street you'd be surprised how many people wanna have a hand in it.

YOUNGBLOOD: I found that out. Even if it ain't in the street people wanna put it there.

BECKER: See you're learning. Soon you gonna know as much as I do. You and Turnbo getting along all right? He been in here?

YOUNGBLOOD: Yeah. We all right. Some man from J&L called here for you. He wants you to call him back. Name of Glucker, I think. Something like that.

BECKER: If you see Doub or Turnbo or Fielding, tell them we gonna have a meeting tonight at seven o'clock. See what we can do about them boarding up the place.

YOUNGBLOOD: Okay, I'll tell them. Come on, baby, before you be late for class.

(*Youngblood and Rena exit. Becker crosses to the phone and dials.*)

BECKER (*Into the phone*): Mr. Glucker in Personnel. (*Pause*) Jim Becker. (*Pause*) Mr. Glucker? Becker here. (*Pause*) When? (*Pause*) Sure I'll be glad to do it for you. (*Pause*) All right. That's no problem. You can count on me. Say, Glucker, I got a young man that's trying to do something with his life, trying to straighten himself out. I wanna send him over to see you. (*Pause*) Well, that'll help. Even something temporary let him show you what kind of worker he is. Thanks. I'll send him over to see you. His name is Robert Shealy. All right now. Thanks again.

(*He hangs up the phone and busies himself with straightening up the station. Booster enters.*)

The station's closed. Ain't no cars here. You might go up on Webster, corner of Roberts. Maceo Brown got a station up there.

BOOSTER: I been thinking about what you said. So many things to think about. After twenty years I thought I got good at thinking . . . but there's so many things you miss. I went out and visited Mama's grave . . .

(*Becker ignores Booster. He gathers up his papers and things and exits the station. Booster is stunned. He gathers himself together and starts to exit when Fielding enters.*)

FIELDING: I just saw your daddy. He must have went on a trip. How you doing?

BOOSTER: Fine. I'm doing fine. Just trying to figure out what to do.

FIELDING: If you in the treetop you can't do nothing but jump to the ground. But first you got to know how you got up there. Did you climb up to get some apples or was you run up by a bear? You got to know that 'cause you might have to start running when you hit the ground. If you trying to figure out what to do . . . you got to first figure out how you got in the situation you in. That's something simple. But you be surprised how many people can't figure that out. *(Looks at Booster's suit)* Is that what they give you? They ought to be ashamed of themselves. That cheap-ass wool ain't but a dollar ninety-nine cents a yard. They could have give you a nice wool gabardine. A good-looking young man like you . . . they could look at you and tell you a connoisseur of fine haberdashery. *(Looks at the suit again with the experienced eye of a tailor)* I could open up them armpits . . . add some new shoulder pads . . . move them buttons . . . lay a double-cross top stitch on that lapel . . . everybody don't know that double-cross top stitch. Ain't but so many fellows can make a double-cross top stitch. At one time in the whole city of Pittsburgh there wasn't but two. Me and Jimmy Green. And he couldn't make it but so good.

BOOSTER: I see you know something about it.

FIELDING: I used to make suits for Billy Eckstine. I used to make all his clothes. He wouldn't let nobody else make them. He get out there on the road and them fellows in the bands be jealous of him. They used to try and outdo each other, you know. Used to try and keep the name of their tailors secret. Count Basie found out I was Billy Eckstine's tailor . . . come through here and wouldn't leave till I had made him a suit. Fucked up his whole tour. Had to cancel Cleveland and Cincinnati while he waited them ten days for that suit. Cost him twenty thousand dollars in lost revenue but he say he didn't care. He tried to steal me away from Billy, but Billy was from Pittsburgh and that made us have more of a bond. Even though I must say I liked Basie 'cause he paid well. But that wasn't enough to tear me and Billy apart. *(Pulls out his bottle and takes a drink)* The only thing that could do that was this here bottle.

That tore a whole lot of things apart. It don't always turn out like you think it is. You don't always have the kind of life that you dream about. You know what I mean?

BOOSTER: I thought I was gonna be the heavyweight champion of the world. Be the next Albert Einstein. But I forgot you can't live in your dreams. I found that out when I was seven. I dreamt I had a bicycle. I went all over on the bicycle. I rode it around in circles. I rode it everywhere. I rode it to the store. I rode it to school. I went all over on the bicycle. Red bicycle. Had a coonskin tail hanging from the handlebars. Had a little bell on the handlebars. Anybody get in your way you just ring that. Had real nice reflectors. Big old seat seem like it too big for you, but then again it seem like it was just big enough. Had fenders in the back . . . a little seat back there in case you want to give somebody a ride they could sit back there. That was one of the nicest bicycles anybody ever wanna see. I woke up and went looking for it. I had to go to school. Where the bike? Why don't I just hop on that? I looked all over for it. I looked in the backyard. The neighbor's yard. Where the bicycle? That's when I decided right then that dreams didn't mean anything in this world. You could be the president or a bishop or something like that. You can dream you got more money than Rockefeller. See what happen when you wake up.

FIELDING: You can dream lucky and wake up cold in hand. That's what my daddy used to say. (Drinks from the bottle) I ain't supposed to do this. I can't let Becker catch me. That's against Becker's rules. I guess you know something about that, huh?

BOOSTER: Something about what?

FIELDING: I say you must know something about Becker's rules.

BOOSTER: Yeah, I guess I do. Becker's rules is what got me in the penitentiary.

FIELDING: I ain't gonna carry it that far.

(*Fielding takes a drink and offers the bottle to Booster, who takes a swig and hands the bottle back to Fielding. Booster crosses to the door.*)

BOOSTER: I'll see you around. (*Exits*)

(*Fielding takes another nip. Philmore enters. He carries a duffel bag. He looks closely at Fielding.*)

PHILMORE: Do I know you?

FIELDING: I know you. I know you live out in Homewood above the Frankstown Bar 'cause I done carried you out there a couple times.

PHILMORE: I used to live out there. My old lady put me out. She don't know but she gonna be missing me. Come next week she gonna be begging me to come back. You watch.

FIELDING: I don't doubt it.

PHILMORE: I went to my sister but she wouldn't let me stay there. Now I got to go to my mama's.

FIELDING: Mama will take you in.

PHILMORE: How much you charge to go out to East Liberty?

FIELDING: That cost three dollars.

PHILMORE: Look here, I ain't got but two dollars. Carry me out there I'll give it to you. I work down there at the William Penn Hotel. I been working down there six years. Never missed a day. Let me owe you a dollar. I'll give it to you next week.

FIELDING: All right. Come on.

PHILMORE: Mama don't like to see you coming . . . but she will take you in.

FIELDING: You got to have somebody you can count on. Now you take my wife. I ain't seen that woman in twenty-two years. I had a dream once . . .

(*Fielding and Philmore exit as the phone rings. The lights go down on the scene.*)

SCENE 2

The lights come up on the jitney station, early evening. Turnbo, Fielding, Youngblood and Doub sit in a circle listening to Becker. The lights and postures of the men convey the idea of a clandestine meeting.

BECKER: All right . . . you all know why we're here. You all know what's happening. The city's fixing to board up the place come the first of the month. They gonna tear it down. They gonna tear the whole block down.

YOUNGBLOOD: They gonna tear the whole neighborhood down.

DOUB: They supposed to build some houses. That's what they need to do.

TURNBO: They supposed to build a new hospital down there on Logan Street. They been talking about that for the longest while. They supposed to build another part to the Irene Kaufmann Settlement House to replace the part they tore down. They supposed to build some houses down on Dinwiddie.

BECKER: Turnbo's right. They *supposed* to build some houses but you ain't gonna see that. You ain't gonna see nothing but the tear-down. That's all I ever seen.

YOUNGBLOOD: That's all there is to see.

FIELDING: They built that senior citizen high-rise on Bedford.

YOUNGBLOOD: We ain't talking about no one building. We talking about the neighborhood.

BECKER: All right. Since they boarding up the place we got to figure out what we gonna do. I talked to Tanenhill about renting that place down on Centre what used to be Siegal's egg store. We can do that. Or we can try to get on with another station. We can go on and play by their rules like we have been. When I first come along I tried to do everything right. I figured that was the best thing to do. Even when it didn't look like they was playing fair I told myself they would come around. Time it look like you got a little something going for you they would change the rules. Now you got to do something else. I told myself that's all right, my boy's coming. He's gonna straighten it out. I put it on somebody else. I took it off of me and put it on somebody else. I told myself as long as I could do that then I could just keep going along and making excuses for everybody. But I'm through making excuses for anybody . . . including myself. I ain't gonna pass it on. I say we stay here. We already here. The people know we here. We been here for eighteen years . . . and I don't see no reason to move. City or no city. I look around and all I see is boarded-up buildings. Some of them been boarded up for more than ten years. If they want to build some houses that's when they can tear it down. When they ready to build the houses. They board this place up the first of the month and let it sit boarded up for the next fifteen . . . twenty years.

TURNBO: That's just how they put Memphis Lee out of business.

BECKER: And if we don't do something they'll put Clifford out of business. Put Hester out of business. Put us out of business. Let Clifford go on and sell his fish sandwich till they get ready to build something. Let Hester go on and sell her milk and butter. 'Cause we gonna run jitneys out of here till the day before the bulldozer come! Ain't gonna be no boarding up around here!

(*The men give cries of approval.*)

We gonna fight them on that. Let them go board up somewhere else.

FIELDING: Sounds good to me.

TURNBO: Come to think of it . . . what they gonna do about it? If we say no, we ain't moving. What they gonna do about it?

FIELDING: If everybody stick together they can't do nothing.

BECKER: We gonna have to raise the dues ten dollars a month . . .

YOUNGBLOOD: Why?

BECKER: To help pay our legal fees. We gonna get us a lawyer. We going in with Clifford and Hester and get us a lawyer. Do it legal. There's ways to fight them. If we gonna be running jitneys out of here we gonna do it right. We get us a lawyer he can go down to the court and file a petition. Now there's a couple things that come up we need to take care of. I want all the cars inspected. The people got a right if you hauling them around in your car to expect the brakes to work. Clean out your trunk. Clean out the interior of your car. Keep your car clean. The people want to ride in a clean car. We providing a service to the community. We ain't just giving rides to people. We providing a service. That's why you answer the phone, "Car service." You don't say, "Becker's Cabs" or "Joe's Jitneys." Part of that service is providing people with a way to get their groceries home or to get their suitcase down to the bus station or the airport so they can go home to visit their mama or whoever it is they want to visit. I want everybody to pull their weight and provide the service that's expected of us. (*Looks at his watch*) Time getting away. I got to go down and work at J&L . . . they got caught shorthanded and need somebody who knows how to operate them machines . . . I'll be over there every night this week. But remember . . . come next week . . . come Tuesday . . . ain't no plywood going up around here. Ain't gonna be no boarding up this station! Youngblood . . . (*Takes a dollar out of his pocket*) Run over Hester's and get us a lightbulb for that lamp.

(*Youngblood exits.*)

DOUB: Hey Becker, what lawyer we gonna get?

BECKER: I don't know, Doub. I ain't thought too much about it.

TURNBO: We ought to get Wendell Freeman. He the one who won that suit for the NAACP when they wouldn't let no colored in them houses out there in Shadyside. As much money as he made on that . . . he ought to work for free.

FIELDING: How you figure he ought to work for free? Who you know work for free? Go ahead . . . name anybody. Who you know work for free?

TURNBO: I wasn't talking to you, Fielding.

DOUB: Whoever it is ought to be on our side. Half the time they be worried about what the city gonna say or think about them. I seen that happen.

BECKER: Yeah, I have too. You can bet whoever we get gonna be on our side. We ain't going through all of this for nothing. Let me get on over to the mill before the shift start. Say Doub . . . oh, never mind. I'll see you tomorrow. (*Exits*)

TURNBO: I'm going over and see what Clifford has to say about them boarding up his place.

DOUB: Here . . . I'll go over with you. (*Crosses to the door*) You coming, Fielding?

(*Fielding indicates a lack of interest.*)

Come on, I'll buy you a fish sandwich.

FIELDING: Oh yeah . . . since you put it like that.

(*Doub and Turnbo exit. Fielding takes a bottle of whiskey from his pocket and starts to take a drink, then changes his mind.*)

A little lemonade never killed nobody. (*Exits*)

(*The lights go down on the scene.*)

SCENE 3

The lights come up on the jitney station, the following day. Doub and Turnbo sit in chairs. Fielding leans against the wall by the phone. Everyone is silent and in a solemn mood. The silence swells. Fielding breaks the silence.

FIELDING: Becker was all right by me. We had our run-ins and all, but he was all right by me. *(The phone rings. Answering it)* Hello? *(Pause)* Yeah. *(Pause)* All right. Be right there. *(Hangs up the phone)* I got a trip. *(Exits)*

TURNBO: When is the funeral, you know?

DOUB: It ain't been set yet.

TURNBO: I wonder if he had any insurance.

DOUB: What you care whether the man had any insurance!

TURNBO: I was just wondering. I'm allowed to wonder. I got something on my mind I just say it. Ain't nothing wrong . . .

DOUB: Turnbo, shut up!

TURNBO: Ain't no sense in me staying here and trying to talk to a damn fool! *(Exits)*

(Doub sits staring at the wall. The phone rings.)

DOUB *(Answering the phone)*: Ain't no cars here today.

(He hangs up the phone as Youngblood enters.)

YOUNGBLOOD: Hey, Doub.

DOUB: Youngblood.

YOUNGBLOOD: Where's everybody?

DOUB: Fielding went on a trip.

YOUNGBLOOD: I seen Turnbo out there sitting in his car.

DOUB: He was in here running off at the mouth.

(Youngblood and Doub sit for a moment in silence.)

YOUNGBLOOD: You couldn't find a nicer man than Becker. You
know? Always keeping things straight. Always worried about
somebody else. Always looking out for you.

DOUB: Yeah.

(Shealy enters.)

You heard?

SHEALY: Yeah, I heard it on the news last night. Man work all
them years down there and ain't nothing happened. Retire
. . . and go back to work one day . . . and that's the day the
bolt decides to break. I can't understand it. It don't make
no sense to me. I went to see Lucille and take her some
money. She hit for a quarter a couple of days ago.

DOUB: How's she taking it?

SHEALY: She's taking it pretty good. Considering how it happened. Sudden and all.

DOUB: I'll have to get by and see her.

(Philmore enters. He is sober and somber.)

SHEALY: Hey, Philmore.

PHILMORE: I'm sorry about Mr. Becker. I heard he got killed
in an accident down at the mill. He was a nice man.

DOUB: Yeah. Thanks.

PHILMORE: You all need any pallbearers?

DOUB: As soon as the arrangements are made, I will let you
know. Don't nobody know too much right now.

PHILMORE: If you do . . . let me know. I'll take off work.

DOUB *(Shaking Philmore's hand)*: Thanks, Philmore. Thanks for
coming around.

(Philmore exits.)

SHEALY *(Digging in his pocket)*: Here go ten dollars for flowers.

DOUB: All right.

YOUNGBLOOD: Here's mine.

SHEALY: You know that boy hit for three dollars yesterday.

DOUB: Who?

SHEALY: Becker's boy. Hit on that three nineteen.

DOUB: Anybody seen him?

SHEALY: Lucille say she ain't heard from him.

DOUB: I wonder do he know?

(Fielding enters.)

FIELDING: Hey, Shealy.

DOUB: We taking ten dollars for flowers, Fielding.

(Fielding goes into his pocket and counts out eight dollars to Doub.)

FIELDING: Loan me two dollars, Youngblood.

DOUB: Here, I'll put it with the four dollars you owe me.

(Turnbo enters.)

FIELDING: What four dollars I owe you?

TURNBO: You know you borrowed four dollars off the man the other day. See, Doub, that's why I wouldn't loan him nothing.

FIELDING: I don't know nothing about no four dollars.

DOUB: That's all right, goddamn it! I know! You just give me six back. Give me ten dollars, Turnbo.

TURNBO: Ten dollars for what?

DOUB: For flowers. Everybody's putting in ten dollars.

FIELDING: How the hell you figure I owe you six dollars?

DOUB: I ain't studying you.

TURNBO: Oh, all right. Did Youngblood give you his?

DOUB: Nigger, why don't you mind your business! For one time, huh?

FIELDING: Hey Doub . . . what I got to give you six back for?

TURNBO: This is my business. I want to make sure everybody pay.

DOUB: Let me take care of that.

YOUNGBLOOD: You ain't got to worry about my business.

TURNBO: I ain't worried about your business. I just say . . .

(The door opens and Booster enters. Everybody falls silent.)

BOOSTER: Hey fellas, my old man around? *(Notices something is wrong)* Hey, what's the matter? *(Notices everybody is looking at him)* What you all sitting around looking at me for?

TURNBO: Ain't you heard?

BOOSTER: Heard what?

DOUB: Boy, don't you know your daddy's dead?

(The phone rings. Booster moves toward Doub.)

BOOSTER: Hey man! What you talking about? Huh? What you talking about? *(Turns toward Fielding)* What's he talking about my daddy dead? *(Moves toward Doub)* What you talking about, man?

DOUB: He got killed down at the . . .

(Booster punches Doub in the face. Youngblood, Turnbo and Shealy grab Booster.)

BOOSTER: What you talking about, nigger!

(They wrestle Booster to the ground.)

Let me go! Let me go! Let me go! That nigger tell me my daddy's dead! Let me go. That nigger tell me my daddy's dead.

(The lights fade to black.)

SCENE 4

The lights come up on the jitney station. It is three days later. Doub, Youngblood, Turnbo, Fielding and Shealy are sitting around. They have just come back from the funeral.

DOUB: When you moving, Youngblood?

YOUNGBLOOD: Saturday.

SHEALY: I hear you bought a house in Penn Hills.

YOUNGBLOOD: Yeah.

SHEALY: They got some nice houses out there. Some of them boys play for the Steelers got houses out there. Them some nice houses.

TURNBO: They ain't as nice as the houses in Monroeville. Most people don't even buy houses in Penn Hills no more. They go out to Monroeville.

SHEALY: Let me see now . . . where you say your house was again? Which one did you buy? I keep forgetting.

YOUNGBLOOD: Reverend Flowers preached a pretty funeral.

FIELDING: Sure did. Made me want to join the church. Have somebody preach over me like that.

TURNBO: The only thing he can say about you is you an alcoholic.

FIELDING: I ain't studying you. Sure I drink. Everybody drink. You ought not to go around calling people names.

DOUB: Why don't you all hold up on that bickering back and forth. Don't nobody wanna hear that today.

SHEALY: You all still gonna stay here? You gonna fight them on boarding up the place, Doub?

TURNBO: What you worried for? The only thing is you won't have no place to take numbers. That's all you worried about.

SHEALY: I was talking to this man right here.

DOUB: I don't know, Shealy. It just wouldn't be the same without Becker.

FIELDING: Naw. Sure wouldn't.

YOUNGBLOOD: I'm ready if everybody else is. If not I'll find a job somewhere. Go to school. Raise my family. Do whatever I have to. You know.

FIELDING: Becker was all right by me. We had our run-ins. But he was all right by me.

(The door opens, and Booster enters.)

BOOSTER: I just wanted to stop by and thank you all for everything you done.

(Booster crosses to Doub, shakes his hand, and puts his arm around him.)

DOUB: Sure. Ain't a man here wouldn't have done anything he could for Becker.

BOOSTER: Yeah, I know.

FIELDING: That's right. You can be proud of your daddy. He was all right by me. I ain't knowed him to have an enemy in the world. Ain't that right, Doub?

BOOSTER: I never knew him too much, you know. I never got to know him like you all did. I can't say nothing wrong by him. He took care of me when I was young. He ain't run the streets and fuss and fight with my mama. The only thing I ever knew him to do was work hard. It didn't matter to me too much at the time 'cause I couldn't see it like I see it now. He had his ways. I guess everybody do. The only thing I feel sorry about . . . is he ain't got out of life what he put in. He deserved better than what life gave him. I can't help thinking that. But you right . . . I'm proud of my old man. I'm proud of him. *(The phone rings)* And I'm proud to be Becker's boy. *(Stops and catches himself)* I didn't come here to preach no sermon.

(*Booster starts toward the door. He stops and turns around. The phone continues to ring. He crosses to it and picks up the receiver.*)

(*Answering the phone*) Car service.

(*The lights fade to black.*)

END OF PLAY

AUGUST WILSON

APRIL 27, 1945–OCTOBER 2, 2005

August Wilson authored *Gem of the Ocean, Joe Turner's Come and Gone, Ma Rainey's Black Bottom, The Piano Lesson, Seven Guitars, Fences, Two Trains Running, Jitney, King Hedley II* and *Radio Golf*. These works explore the heritage and experience of African Americans, decade by decade, over the course of the twentieth century. Mr. Wilson's plays have been produced at regional theaters across the country, on Broadway and throughout the world. In 2003, Mr. Wilson made his professional stage debut in his one-man show *How I Learned What I Learned*.

Mr. Wilson's work garnered many awards, including the Pulitzer Prize for *Fences* (1987) and *The Piano Lesson* (1990); a Tony Award for *Fences*; Great Britain's Olivier Award for *Jitney*; and eight New York Drama Critics Circle awards for *Ma Rainey's Black Bottom, Fences, Joe Turner's Come and Gone, The Piano Lesson, Two Trains Running, Seven Guitars, Jitney* and *Radio Golf*. Additionally, the cast recording of *Ma Rainey's Black Bottom* received a 1985 Grammy Award, and Mr. Wilson received a 1995 Emmy Award nomination for his screenplay adaptation of *The Piano Lesson*. Mr. Wilson's early works include the one-act plays: *The Janitor, Recycle, The Coldest Day of the Year, Malcolm X, The Homecoming* and the musical satire *Black Bart and the Sacred Hills*.

Mr. Wilson received many fellowships and awards, including Rockefeller and Guggenheim fellowships in playwriting, the Whiting Writers Award and the 2003 Heinz Award. He was awarded a 1999 National Humanities Medal by the President of the United States, and received numerous honorary degrees from colleges and universities, as well as the only high school diploma ever issued by the Carnegie Library of Pittsburgh.

He was an alumnus of New Dramatists, a member of the American Academy of Arts and Sciences, a 1995 inductee into the American Academy of Arts and Letters, and on October 16, 2005, Broadway renamed the theater located at 245 West 52nd Street: The August Wilson Theatre. In 2007, he was posthumously inducted into the Theater Hall of Fame.

Mr. Wilson was born and raised in the Hill District of Pittsburgh, and lived in Seattle at the time of his death. He is survived by two daughters, Sakina Ansari and Azula Carmen Wilson, and his wife, costume designer Constanza Romero.